D1006263

CAREERS IN THE US AIR FORCE

Earle Rice Jr. and Wilson Camelo

Enslow Publishing
101 W. 23rd Street
Suite 240
New York, NY 10011
USA
enslow.com

Published in 2016 by Enslow Publishing, LLC
101 W. 23rd Street, Suite 240, New York, NY 10011

Library of Congress Cataloging-in-Publication Data
Rice, Earle.
Careers in the Air Force / Earle Rice Jr. and Wilson Camelo.
pages cm. — (Careers in the US Armed Forces)
Includes bibliographical references and index.
Summary: "Describes many careers in the US Air Force"—Provided by publisher.
Audience: Grades 7 to 8.
ISBN 978-0-7660-6941-1
1. United States. Air Force—Juvenile literature. 2. United States. Air Force—Vocational guidance—Juvenile literature. I. Camelo, Wilson. II. Title.
UG633.R3926 2015
358.4023'73—dc23
2015012794

Printed in the United States of America

To Our Readers: We have done our best to make sure all Web site addresses in this book were active and appropriate when we went to press. However, the author and the publisher have no control over and assume no liability for the material available on those Web sites or on any Web sites they may link to. Any comments or suggestions can be sent by e-mail to customerservice@enslow.com.

Portions of this book originally appeared in the book *The U.S. Air Force and Military Careers*.

Photo Credits: Afro American Newspapers/Gado/Archive Photo/Getty Images, p. 63; AFP/Getty Images, p. 29; Air Force TSGT Jose Lopez/US Air Force/Wikimedia Commons/Three F-5E Tiger II from 527th Tactical Fighter Training Aggressor Squadron.jpg/public domain, p. 102; © AP Images, p. 6; Christine Yarusi, p. 1 (series logo); Daniel Bendjy/E+/Getty Images, p. 1 (Air Force uniform and stethoscope); Derrick Goode/US Air Force/Getty Images, p. 37; ERIC FEFERBERG/AFP/Getty Images, p. 38; FPG/Archive Photos/Getty Images, p. 59; Hulton Archive/Getty Images, p. 16; Interim Archives/Archive Photos/Getty Images, p. 24; Keystone/Hulton Archive/Getty Images, p. 20; KEN MANN/US Air Force/Wikimedia Commons/McGuire Aire Force Base.jpg/ public domain, p. 72; Miaow Miaow/US Air Force/Wikimedia Commons/USAF F-16A F-15C F-15E Desert Storm pic.jpg/public domain, p. 32; NASA photo, p. 51; Paul Hakimata Photograph/Shutterstock.com, p. 1 (woman); © PF-(sdasm1)/Alamy, p. 66; Photo by Master Sgt. Lee Roberts, USAF/DoD, p. 44; Pictorial Parade/Archive Photos/Getty Images, p. 14; RAMZI HAIDAR/AFP/Getty Images, p. 36; Siri Stafford/Digital Vision/Thinkstock, p. 1 (man); Staff Sgt. Aaron Allmon II/US Air Force/Wikimedia Commons/F-117 Nighthawk Front.jpg/public domain, p. 31; Steve Cukrov/Shutterstock.com (chapter openers); USAF photo by Alan Boedeker, p. 49; US Air Force photo, pp. 60, 106; US Air Force photo/Airman 1st Class Erin R. Babis, p. 124; US Air Force photo by Airman 1st Class Bradly A Lail, p. 99; US Air Force photo by Airman 1st Class Taylor Queen, p. 75; US Air Force photo by Judson Brohmer/Wikimedia Commons/F-22 Raptor lauching AIM-9 Sidewinder - 021105-O-9999G-072.jpg/public domain, p. 35; US Air Force photo by Lt. Col. Bill Ramsay, p. 4; US Air Force photo/Master Sgt. Jessica Kendziorek, p. 94; US Air Force photo/Ray McCoy, p. 83; US Air Force photo/Rick Berry, p. 73; US Air Force photo/Robbin Cresswell, p. 78; US Air Force photo by Senior Airman Camilla Elizeu/defenseimagery.mil/Wikimedia Commons/US Air Force 1st. Lt. Garrett Sinclair, a current operations officer with the 79th Rescue Squadron, schedules training flights Sept 130904-F-ML420-001.jpg/public domain, p. 97; US Air Force photo/Senior Airman Clay Lancaster, p. 104; US Air Force photo /Senior Airman Nichelle Anderson, p. 74; US Air Force photo / Staff Sgt. Bennie Davis III, p. 91; US Air Force photo/Staff Sgt. Gustavo Gonzalez, p. 54; US Air Force photo by Staff Sgt. Marleah Robertson, p. 96; US Air Force/Tech. Sgt. Jason Lake, p. 39; US Air Force photo by Tech Sgt. Thomas J. Doscher, p. 45; US Air National Guard photo by Tech. Sgt. Caycee Watson, p. 42; © ZUMA Press, Inc/Alamy.

Cover Credits: Daniel Bendjy/E+/Getty Images (Air Force uniform and stethoscope); Paul Hakimata Photograph/Shutterstock.com (African-American woman); Siri Stafford/Digital Vision/Thinkstock (African-American man); Ethan Miller/Getty Images News/Getty Images (bottom); Christine Yarusi (series logo).

CONTENTS

MA

OUT OF THE FLAMES

It was autumn in New York City. The sky was clear and bright blue. Leaves had begun to fall, and the air was crisp with seasonal change. If there is ever such a thing as a perfect day, this was one—a day to remember. But for all the wrong reasons.

American Airlines Flight 11 slammed into the North Tower of the World Trade Center at 8:46:40 AM. Most federal agencies learned of the crash from watching CNN. In Sarasota, Florida, a presidential motorcade was just arriving at Emma E. Booker Elementary School. President George W. Bush was scheduled to read to a class and talk about education. While standing just outside the classroom, Senior Advisor to the president Karl Rove informed President Bush that a small, twin-engine plane had crashed into the World Trade Center. The president's initial reaction was to attribute the happening to pilot error.

Moments later, while the president was seated in the classroom at 9:05, White House Chief of Staff Andrew Card whispered to him: "A second plane hit the second tower. America is under attack."[1] President Bush remained outwardly calm so as not to alarm the children. Five to seven minutes later, he retired to a holding room. His staff briefed him as he watched television coverage of the world-changing event. It was September 11, 2001.

By 9:45, Bush was on board Air Force One and was using the Air Force's secure communications to speak with Vice President Dick Cheney at the White House. There was much confusion in the early hours of the attack as to how many hijacked planes were still in the air or if Air Force One was a target.

After being whisked away to Louisiana and Nebraska for secret meetings following the terrorist attacks, President Bush returned to Andrews Air Force base.

President's Pilot

Colonel Mark Tillman (Ret.) landed Air Force One in Saratoga, Florida, on September 10, 2001. A decade later, in an interview with *Arizona Republic* reporter Dennis Wagner, he reminisced about the events of the following day. Tillman had been with Air Force One since 1992 and had been promoted to chief presidential pilot earlier in 2001. He had just arrived at the airport on the morning of 9/11 when he learned that a plane had flown into one of the towers at the World Trade Center. His boss ordered him to leave Sarasota as soon as the president got aboard. "I thought we should fly to a secure base along the East Coast, or to Camp David," Tillman recalled. "Nobody took into account that a proud Texan would be in office. He wanted to fly straight to the nation's capital—to go back and fight."[2] After brief diversions to Air Force bases in Louisiana and Nebraska, President George W. Bush looked at his pilot and said, "Tillman, let's go home."[3] They picked up F-16 escorts along the way. "Nine hours after the ordeal began," Tillman said, "we landed at Andrews and the crew heaved a collective sigh of relief."[4]

The president authorized the military to shoot down any civilian aircraft that was a threat. The staff at First Air Force (1st AF) at Tyndall Air Force Base in Florida began coordinating the aerial response with the North American Aerospace Defense Command (NORAD) at Peterson Air Force Base, Colorado. Together, 1st AF and NORAD are responsible for patrolling and defending American airspace.

Air Force fighter jets, such as F-15s from Langley Air Force Base in Virginia, were soon streaking across the sky responding to the attacks. One headed toward a hijacked aircraft thought to be targeting Washington, D.C. However, before the F-15 arrived, the plane crashed in western Pennsylvania after passengers fought back for control of the aircraft. Other jet fighters were sent to provide air cover, called Combat Air Patrols, over cities like New York and Washington, D.C.

Even more Air Force aircraft and units also responded to the attacks. A C-5 cargo aircraft from Westover Air Reserve Base in Massachusetts, on its way to Australia, was rerouted to Travis Air Force Base in California to pick up a search-and-rescue unit and bring its members to New York City to search the World Trade Center rubble for survivors.

While the public does not know all its specific protective capabilities, Air Force One has many defensive systems. However, rather than take risks, when Air Force One took off from Florida, it flew at a very high altitude where it had a better chance of outrunning a civilian airliner.[5] Air Force crews took Bush to Barksdale Air Force Base in Louisiana. There, he made several phone calls from a conference room to Vice President Cheney, Defense Secretary Donald Rumsfeld, and New York senator Charles Schumer. At the base, President Bush made a speech, assuring America that security measures were being taken.[6]

Air Force One then left Barksdale and went to Offutt Air Force Base in Nebraska. The president and staff went to the base's command post deep underground. After a one-hour meeting, Bush reboarded Air Force One. With F-16 fighter aircraft flying protective cover, he returned to Andrews Air Force Base where he boarded a helicopter to the White House. As he approached the White House, the president could see the Pentagon, which also had been hit by a hijacked civilian airliner that day. "The mightiest building in the world is on fire," he said.[7]

Out of the flames, a new Air Force emerged. From that day on, the Air Force would change. It would have a more direct role in defending the homeland from aerial attack in the War on Terrorism. However, the Air Force would need a different mentality to respond to the battles it would face in the twenty-first century. The enemy would no longer directly challenge the Air Force in the air: it would be nimbler, using terrorist tactics and blending into society.

THE WINGS OF WAR

"If the wheels of time could be turned back," Wilbur Wright wrote a friend in 1906, "it is not at all probable we would do again what we have done. . . . It was due to a peculiar combination of circumstances which might never occur again."[1] Wilbur was being modest. Between 1899 and 1903, he and his brother Orville, two sons of Ohio, had spent most of their time on a lonely beach on a remote island off the North Carolina coast. They set up camp near Kitty Hawk at the base of a barren sandhill called Big Kill Devil Hill. There they built gliders and experimented with airfoils and control surfaces. With lessons learned, they advanced to the theory of aerial propulsion and added a twelve horsepower engine to their glider. On December 17, 1903, Orville lifted their fragile craft off the ground for twelve seconds. Wilbur followed later with a flight lasting fifty-nine seconds. They had solved the enigma of powered heavier-than-air flight. And the world entered the Age of Flight.

The Wright brothers were not the first to fly a heavier-than-air craft. For more than a century, people had flown in balloons and gliders. The problem was not getting in the air; it was getting in the air when one wanted and steering and landing safely.[2]

In 1908, the US Army invested in a steerable airship, called a dirigible, which could stay in the air for two hours and fly at a rate of 20 miles per hour.[3] Later that year, Orville Wright piloted a plane during a demonstration for Army authorities. Unfortunately, the plane crashed, killing a signal corpsman, Lieutenant Thomas Selfridge. He was the first US military aviation casualty.[4]

However, many in the United States did not recognize the military use for airplanes, so the Wright brothers went to Europe to promote their accomplishment. British, French, German, and Italian military forces quickly adopted aircraft into their arsenals.

The US Army finally purchased its first airplane from the Wright brothers in 1909.[5] The Wright brothers trained the first military pilots. Even though they successfully used rifles and bombs to shoot targets from a plane, the Army did not think aircraft could do more than reconnaissance, or checking on the enemy's position. In 1912, the Army announced it would no longer fund aviation experiments.

As a result, airplanes were not used in combat until 1916 when General John Pershing led an unsuccessful mission to find and capture Mexican revolutionary Pancho Villa. But war was ravaging much of Europe, and aviation would play an important role on the continent.

First Army Air Service

World War I, the "war to end all wars," had been fought for almost three years when the United States entered it in April 1917. American aviation forces had only 131 officers, of whom just 26 were considered fully trained. There were no combat aircraft, no units trained in warfare, and no pilots with combat experience. European pilots already had three years' experience.[6]

The United States had no plans to build an air service that could fight in Europe or any capabilities to quickly build fighter aircraft. In the year before America entered the war, civilian factories had only delivered 64 of the 366 planes ordered. On May 24, 1917, President Woodrow Wilson received a telegram from French Premier Alexandre Ribot requesting that America send 4,500 planes and 5,000 pilots to the front by spring 1918. The request helped start the Army's aviation expansion.[7]

In Europe, American pilots trained with their Allied partners and flew reconnaissance missions in the fall of 1918. On the morning of October 5, 1918, the 50th Aero Squadron observation unit was on a mission to find and bring supplies to three battalions of the 77th Division. Flying low in fog and hostile fire, the unit went searching for a missing battalion. They dropped supplies where they thought the battalion was, but the supplies were gathered up by the Germans.[8]

The next morning, Lieutenants Harold Goettler and Erwin Bleckley took off in their DH-4 aircraft to continue searching. They returned to where they thought the battalion was located, but came under attack. The lieutenants flew back to the airfield for repairs and returned again to the area, but German gunners were waiting. Goettler and Bleckley were attacked and were shot down and killed. They were later awarded the Medal of Honor. The day after the pilots were killed, survivors of the "Lost Battalion," as they came to be known, were located.[9]

Perhaps the best-known American World War I era aviation commander was General William "Billy" Mitchell. Concerned that inexperienced units were being sent into combat, Mitchell took control of training the First Army Air Service. He soon had under his control the largest group of air forces ever assembled in a single operation during World War I. Mitchell's 1,481 aircraft and 30,000 men came from American, French, Italian, and British forces and were likely the first aerial coalition.[10]

The First Army Air Service's first battle took place from September 12 to September 16 with impressive results. American pilots made thirty-three hundred flights over enemy lines, fired thirty thousand rounds, made more than one thousand bomb attacks destroying twelve enemy balloons and sixty planes.[11] The battle also produced the first two American aces (pilots who down more than five enemy aircraft), Captain Eddie Rickenbacker and Second Lieutenant Frank Luke.

The last American air victory of World War I occurred on November 10, 1918, when Major Maxwell Kirby shot down a German Fokker while flying his Spad-13 on a patrol mission. Kirby attacked the unsuspecting German from above and fired his machine gun within fifty feet.[12] The war ended the next day.

Overall, American aviators were credited with destroying 776 enemy planes and 72 enemy balloons. They took more

Fighter pilot Eddie Rickenbacker was one of America's first two flying aces during World War I.

than 18,000 photographs and dropped 275,000 pounds of bombs. They lost 290 planes and 37 balloons. They also had 569 battle casualties, 164 aviators killed in action, 102 captured, and 200 missing in action.[13]

Between Two World Wars

America learned many lessons about airpower during the First World War, and military commanders soon began to develop ways to fight future air wars. Mitchell returned from Europe ready to play a role in shaping the future of airpower only to discover his position as director of Military Aeronautics was eliminated by Chief of the Air Service, General Charles Menoher. In addition, Congress reduced the Air Service from two hundred thousand people to only ten thousand. General Menoher told manufacturers that "not a dollar is available for the purchase of new aircraft."[14] The aviation budget projected for $83 million was cut to only $25 million; meanwhile, the British increased their spending to $350 million.[15]

Mitchell criticized these actions and believed in the need for a separate air force. He bragged to Congress that he could sink or destroy any Navy ship, and that for the cost of one battleship they could buy one thousand bombers. Congress ordered the Navy to provide Mitchell with old ships he could use in a test. The Navy thought Mitchell would fail. Secretary of the Navy Josephus Daniel said, "I am so confident that neither the Army nor Navy aviators can hit the Iowa when she is underway that I would be perfectly willing to be on board her when they bomb her."[16]

In February 1921, Mitchell gathered nearly one thousand men and two hundred fifty airplanes at Langley Field in

The captured German battleship *Ostfriesland* is bombed by US Army Air Corps aircraft during tests on the effects of aerial bombing on warships on June 21, 1921.

Virginia to practice. The test came on June 21, using the German battleship *Ostfriesland* as a target ship, which had been turned over to the United States after World War I. The Navy considered the ship "unsinkable." However, in only twenty-two minutes, the planes bombed and sank the *Ostfriesland*. Mitchell earned instant fame around the world.[17]

Mitchell soon went to the Pacific to gather information. He found poor cooperation between the intelligence services. The growth in Japanese industry, and the increase in their air power, concerned him enough to predict that one day the Japanese would attack Pearl Harbor from the air. When he returned to the United States in 1924, he found the

Air Service was still in poor shape, and his predictions about Japan were not taken seriously. Mitchell continued voicing his disagreements with the War Department until President Calvin Coolidge ordered him court-martialed.[18]

The trial lasted seven weeks, but the jury took only forty minutes to find Mitchell guilty on all charges. He was sentenced to a reduced rank and loss of all pay for five years. He retired instead. Mitchell was later vindicated when many of his predictions about airpower came true, including the one about Pearl Harbor.

Prelude to the Nuclear Age

By the time Japanese Lieutenant Akira Sakamoto dropped the first Japanese bomb on Pearl Harbor on December 7, 1941, the military role of airpower was well established. At the time of the attack, there were 231 Army Air Force planes in Hawaii. Some were considered fighter aircraft and others, like the B-17, were bombers. However, less than half of the aircraft were considered fully operational.[19]

In fact, it was a flight of B-17s on the way to Oahu early that morning that confused Lieutenant Kermit Tyler, who did not realize the strange "blips" on the radar were Japanese attack aircraft. With the attack, the United States was thrust into World War II in the Pacific. The Japanese continued their aggressive attacks throughout the South Pacific. However, at the time, US aircraft did not have enough range to reach Japan from Hawaii.

In April 1942, the United States would have a small measure of revenge through an innovative air strike on mainland Japan. Lieutenant Colonel Jimmy Doolittle created a plan to launch B-25 bombers from the deck of the Navy carrier Hornet. Volunteers were found and only informed they would be flying the most dangerous mission of their lives. Crews trained at Eglin Field in Florida by flying off a patch of airstrip marked with the width and length of the Hornet's deck.[20]

The plan was to launch the B-25s about four hundred miles from the Japanese coast, have them bomb sites in Japan, and then land in either China or Russia. Landing in Japan would have meant an instant execution. Most of the B-25's guns and equipment were removed to make them as light as possible to conserve fuel.

However, on the day of the attack, April 18, 1942, the Hornet was spotted by a Japanese boat, and the attack had to take place from 650 miles away.[21] Doolittle led the attack and was the pilot of the first B-25 to take off from the Hornet. The B-25s struck Tokyo and other Japanese cities. Many B-25 crews, low on fuel, bailed out, killing one crewman. Only one B-25 landed safely in the Soviet Union. Three aircraft came down in Japanese-occupied China and the crews were later executed. While the damage to Japan was not severe, the attack gave the enemy a jolt and the American people a much-needed morale boost. Doolittle was promoted to brigadier general and later awarded the Medal of Honor.

In Europe, Army Air Force aircraft and personnel were sent to fight with the allies against Germany. Again, bombers would play a significant role in turning the tide and ending the war.

One key to defeating Germany was destroying its military industrial capabilities, like ball-bearing factories. The bombing was highly inaccurate, the weather in Europe was poor, and bombers had to fly to their targets at very high altitudes to avoid antiaircraft artillery. As a result, hundreds of bombers were often needed on a single mission to destroy a target. In addition, fighter escorts did not have enough fuel to escort the bombers all the way to the target. Many bombers were shot down. Morale was low among bomber pilots. The War Department started a policy that allowed bomber crews who successfully flew twenty-five consecutive missions to return home. The first crew to do this was from the *Memphis Belle*, named for a crewmember's girlfriend.

On June 6, 1944, the United States launched the D-Day invasion against German forces in Europe. Air forces conducted bombing missions ahead of American ground troops that were attacking in places like Normandy, France. Fighters provided aerial support for invading troops, cargo aircraft carried critical supplies, and other planes dropped paratroopers behind enemy lines. The end result of the massive invasion was Germany's surrender on May 8, 1945, also called V-E day.

Ciao Francesco

Corporal Frank Medina of the Army Air Force was a tail gunner on a B-24 when his aircraft was shot down over Italy. He and the crew parachuted out of the plane and landed in a cornfield. Dodging machine-gun fire, he was trapped behind enemy lines for eight months. He survived by using his military training and assistance from friendly Italians. His story is well documented in his book *Ciao Francesco*.[22]

Waco gliders of the Ninth Airforce Troop Carrier Command prepare to land on the fields of Northern France on D-Day during World War II.

Fighting in the Pacific continued in Japan and other Pacific islands until B-29 bombers dropped atomic bombs on the Japanese cities of Hiroshima and Nagasaki. World War II was over on August 15, 1945, but, not before more than forty thousand Army Air Force members were killed in action and fifteen thousand in training or accidents in the United States.[23]

Chapter 3: Birth of an Independent Air Force

The idea of an independent air force was first proposed by Billy Mitchell and other forward thinkers in the 1920s. It was advanced during World War II by leaders like Generals Henry H. "Hap" Arnold and Carl "Tooey" Spaatz. On December 19, 1945, President Harry S Truman called on Congress for legislation that would merge the War and Navy departments into a single department of national defense and create a coequal, independent air force. "Air power has been developed to a point where its responsibilities are equal to those of land and sea power," he said, "and its contribution to our strategic planning is as great."[1] At the president's direction, the United States Air Force was born.

The Navy was opposed because they wanted to be solely responsible for protecting the borders of the United States. On September 18, 1947, after the National Security Act was passed, the Air Force was born. W. Stuart Symington became the first secretary of the Air Force, and Carl Spaatz became the first Air Force chief of staff.[2]

The Air Force soon faced a test in Germany. The Soviet Union wanted the Allies to leave a divided Berlin. To counter the Soviets, the Air Force flew thousands of missions to bring aid to the Western half of the city. This massive effort in 1948 was called "The Berlin Airlift."[3]

Air War in the Jet Age

On June 25, 1950, North Korean troops and tanks charged south across the 38th parallel toward Seoul, the capital of the Republic of Korea. War broke out, and the United Nations asked its members to help defend South Korea. Until enough US troops could be deployed in the south, it was the Far Eastern Air Force that largely defended against the aggressors.

The United States had entered the jet era, but it was not the only nation with capable airplanes. The first effective combat jet was the Russian MiG-15.[4] Soon, the Air Force introduced the F-80 Shooting Star and F-86 Sabre to face the Russian fighters in areas known as "MiG Alley," the communist stronghold in northwest Korea.

At first, the Air Force provided defensive support, but on October 7, 1950, President Harry Truman authorized US troops to go after retreating North Korean forces across the 38th parallel. American and South Korean forces entered the North Korean capital of Pyongyang on October 19. Far Eastern Air Force B-29s and B-26s bombed targets in North Korea, while B-26s, F-51s, and F-80s provided close air support to ground troops.[5]

USAF crews in Korea prepare F-86 Sabre jet fighters while they sit on the flight line getting ready for combat.

In 1952, the Air Force replaced many of its F-86Es with F-86Fs, which had more powerful engines and improved wing edges that allowed them to better compete with the MiG-15. The Communists restricted their flights to MiG Alley and often avoided aerial combat with F-86 pilots. By August and September, MiG pilots became more aggressive, and aerial engagements occurred almost daily. However, US pilots had the upper hand. For example, from May to June 1953, F-86F forces claimed 165 aerial victories while losing only 3 aircraft.[6]

After two years of negotiations, the Korean War ended on July 27, 1953. More than fifty-four thousand Americans died in the war.[7] The dividing line between North and South Korea remained at the 38th Parallel, where the two sides had battled to a standstill.

Following the Korean War, the United States entered an arms and space race with the Soviet Union. The Russians were the first to go into space in 1957 when they launched their satellite, Sputnik. They were also the first to put a man into space. The United States followed by putting its own manned spacecraft into orbit, and President John F. Kennedy promised to have a man on the moon by 1969. That occurred during the Richard Nixon presidency, almost six years after Kennedy was assassinated. In addition to space exploration, both Russian- and American-made nuclear missiles were developed and deployed throughout Europe. Both sides kept each other in check through a system called Mutually Assured Destruction, or MAD. It meant each side had enough nuclear weapons to destroy the other side, so neither would benefit by striking first.

In 1962, nuclear war seemed possible when Air Force U-2 spy planes flying over Cuba came back with images of Russian missile sites under construction. If completed, the missiles in Cuba could reach the eastern United States. President Kennedy declared Cuba under quarantine, and established an aerial and naval blockade of supplies to Cuba. The world held its breath. Eventually Russian Premier Nikita Khrushchev backed down.

Thunder in the East

Vietnam was divided in two in 1954 after the French, who had colonized the country, were defeated. The north, a communist regime, and the south, under an anticommunist leader, soon resumed fighting. In 1961, the United States began training the South Vietnamese armed forces and conducting active operations like reconnaissance.[8]

At the end of 1961, President John F. Kennedy's advisors recommended more American involvement in Vietnam. By 1963, there were fifteen thousand Americans in Vietnam. With Lyndon Johnson as president in 1964, the United States began a bombing campaign. However, American leadership in Washington wanted to control the war in Vietnam so they would not lose American support. Leaders in Washington thought that by "sending signals" to the North Vietnamese through limited bombing they would stop hostilities.

However, the North Vietnamese never believed that Americans had enough commitment to be a threat. Although more bombs were dropped on Vietnam than in all of World War II, much of it was not effective because American political leaders did not want to target civilian areas and encourage negative press coverage. Regulations in warfare, called Rules of Engagement (ROE), were established that restricted what Americans could do. For example, at one point Americans could not strike a surface-to-air missile facility unless an actual missile was installed on the launcher and a missile was shot at an American aircraft.

The United States launched an air campaign called "Rolling Thunder" in 1965, using aircraft like the F-105 and the F-4 Phantom to strike targets over cities like Hanoi. The North Vietnamese countered with aircraft like MiG-17s and MiG-21s, but their antiaircraft and surface-to-air missiles were a bigger threat, claiming many US aircraft and crews. In 1966 alone, the Air Force lost 2,257 aircraft.[9]

When Richard Nixon became president in 1969 he continued discussions to end the war. However, he suspended peace talks at one point and authorized a major air campaign called Operation Linebacker. It was the most effective use of American airpower in Vietnam because it took out many of the targets that were previously off-limits for political reasons. When peace talks resumed and then failed again, the Americans launched Operation Linebacker II. Fifteen B-52 bombers were lost during the eleven-day offensive, but according to some air force analysts, it proved what airpower could have achieved during the war if properly used. In January 1973, negotiations to end the war restarted, and an agreement was finally signed. Americans headed home by March. Two years later, the communists in the north unified all of Vietnam under their power.[10]

Shield and Storm

In August 1990, Saddam Hussein's Iraqi military invaded neighboring Kuwait, which is rich with oil and has access to

Loadmaster Levitow

John L. Levitow was a loadmaster on an AC-47 aircraft flying a night mission in Vietnam when it was struck by a mortar round. The explosion ripped a hole through the wing and sent fragments into the fuselage. The whole crew was injured. An explosion tore an activated flare from one crewmember's hand. Levitow, suffering from more than forty fragment wounds, staggered to his feet and saw the smoking flare.

Realizing the plane could catch on fire and crash if the flare ignited inside, Levitow started toward the smoking flare. However, the aircraft was partially out of control so the flare was rolling wildly from side to side and Levitow could not grab it with his hands. Instead, he threw himself on the burning flare. Hugging the flare to his body, he dragged himself to the back of the aircraft and hurled the flare through a cargo door. It ignited safely outside the aircraft. His actions saved the crew from certain death.

the Persian Gulf. A small group of US Air Force fighter jets were the only defense between Saddam's forces and the oil fields of nearby Saudi Arabia.

The United Nations passed a resolution demanding Saddam leave Kuwait or face serious consequences. When he refused, the United States and its allies began Operation Desert Shield. Soon, thousands of US and foreign troops and aircraft deployed to several countries in the Middle East to show Saddam that the world was serious about his forces leaving Kuwait. They also wanted to prevent Iraq from invading other countries.

During the Vietnam War, the Air Force worked with the Navy in Operation Linebacker, a campaign aimed at stopping supplies from reaching North Vietnam.

The Air Force sent some of its newest weapons including the F-117 stealth fighter. It was considered a stealth aircraft since it was designed to deflect and absorb radar. In addition, a new line of "smart bombs" were introduced. They used satellites, radar, and lasers to guide them to a target.

President George H.W. Bush gave Saddam until January 17, 1991, to remove his forces from Kuwait or face a massive attack. The deadline passed and Operation Desert Shield turned into Operation Desert Storm. A wave of F-117 stealth fighters soon entered Iraqi airspace undetected and bombed numerous targets in the Iraqi capital of Baghdad. Although the F-117 had been used before, the Persian Gulf War was the first time the world saw the capabilities of stealth technology.

Air Force fighter and bomber aircraft began hitting Saddam's power plants, bridges, and communications posts. Saddam's forces were essentially left blind, mute, and deaf. Unable to communicate with his generals and forced to sleep in a different location almost every night, Saddam Hussein saw his military fall apart. Thousands of troops surrendered to coalition forces and what was left of Saddam's air force escaped to Iran.

After weeks of aerial bombing, the ground offensive began. It lasted only one hundred hours. Iraqi forces were driven out of Kuwait and Operation Desert Storm was over.

Operation Allied Force

After his election in 1989, Yugoslav President Slobodan Milosevic imposed Serbian rule in Kosovo, a small province within Serbia. He began a campaign of violence against the ethnic Kosovar Albanians, resulting in the death of more than two hundred fifty thousand civilians by 1995.

In 1998, Milosevic ordered an attack against the Albanian guerrilla force called the Kosovo Liberation Army. Some eighty civilians were killed. The United States sent an ambassador to Belgrade to convince Milosevic to stop targeting civilians. When Milosevic refused, the United Nations passed Security Council Resolution 1199 calling for the end of hostilities. Milosevic initially agreed to let a North Atlantic Treaty Organization (NATO) group into Kosovo to monitor compliance, but he continued his violence against the Albanians. Following other attempts to convince Milosevic to negotiate, and armed with U-2 imagery of mass graves in Kosovo, the United States and NATO gave Milosevic an ultimatum.

He refused to comply and war began. This would be no ordinary war, however. Concerned over lack of congressional and NATO support for a ground war, which could result in many combat casualties, President Bill Clinton called for the conflict to be conducted solely from the air. On March 29, 1999, the first all-air conflict, named Operation Allied Force, was launched.

The first phase of the air campaign was to take out the country's integrated air defense system (IADS) and other targets to show that NATO could attack from the air with minimum collateral, or unintended, damage. The mountainous terrain was challenging for bombing and the weather was usually cloudy. This meant precision-guided munitions (PGMs) would be the weapons of choice. In Desert Storm, 10 percent of the aircraft could deliver PGMs, but during Operation Allied Force that number was 90 percent.[11]

Operation Allied Force marked the combat debut of the B-2 stealth bomber, and the first time the Air Force used its

The F-117 Nighthawk was a stealth ground-attack fighter used in the Gulf War.

F-16A, F-15C, and F-15E war planes fly over burning oil wells during Operation Desert Storm in 1991.

three heavy bombers—the B-2, B-52, and B-1—together in combat. All told, they dropped more than eleven thousand out of the more than twenty-three thousand American bombs during the conflict.[12] B-2s flew nonstop to Kosovo from Whiteman Air Force Base in Missouri on missions that lasted around thirty hours to drop satellite-guided bombs on enemy targets.

Stealth technology suffered its first combat loss. Serb missile operators on the ground knew that an F-117 would enter their area and hit the F-117 with a surface-to-air missile when it briefly became visible on radar as it opened its bomb doors. The pilot ejected and was rescued.[13]

On June 9, 1999, Milosevic accepted a peace agreement to allow fifty thousand NATO-led forces into the country. Operation Allied Force was over. In the end, allied crews flew 38,004 sorties in all, of which more than 23,300 were combat missions.

CHAPTER 4

TERROR HITS HOME

On September 20, 2001, at 9 P.M. EDT, President George W. Bush addressed members of Congress and a nation still in collective shock over the dastardly terrorist attacks of September11. To most Americans, terror attacks were obscure events that happened to other people in far off places. But nine days earlier, terror had hit home. Tonight, it was the job of the president to heal a wounded nation and inspire national confidence for the troubled days ahead. He spoke to a nation and a world that had changed forever on 9/11:

> *Great harm has been done to us. We have suffered great loss. And in our grief and anger we have found our mission and our moment. Freedom and fear are at war. The advance of human freedom—the great achievement of our time, and the great hope of every time—now*

depends on us. Our nation—this generation—will lift a dark threat of violence from our people and our future. We will rally the world to this cause by our efforts, by our courage. We will not tire, we will not falter, and we will not fail.

The United States, he said, would not wait to be attacked. This policy would later become known as the Bush Doctrine. In that same speech, he gave an ultimatum to the Taliban government in Afghanistan, which was protecting the Al-Qaeda terrorist group and its leader Osama bin Laden, to close terrorist training camps and hand over terrorists.[1] Al-Qaeda was thought to have been responsible for the September 11 terrorists attacks.

Operation Enduring Freedom

The Taliban refused. On October 7, 2001, the first military strike in the war on terrorism, called Operation Enduring Freedom, began.[2] On the first night of the conflict, B-2 stealth bombers were launched from Whiteman AFB in Missouri on the longest-distance combat mission in the history of aviation. Six B-2s flew forty-four-hour missions to Afghanistan, dropping satellite-guided bombs and landing on Diego Garcia, an island controlled by Britain in the Indian Ocean.[3]

In addition to fighting the Taliban, Air Force aircraft were also involved in helping deliver needed food and medicine to the Afghan people. On February 7, 2002, General Tommy Franks, commander of US Central Command (USCENTCOM), the group responsible for fighting wars in areas like the Middle East, declared Afghanistan was no

An F-22 Raptor fires an AIM-9 Sidewinder missile during an evaluation of how well the fighter plane could launch an air-to-air missile from an internal weapons bay.

longer a safe haven for Al-Qaeda. This was due in part to the work of the US Air Force.[4]

While the main conflict was over, much work was left in Afghanistan—finding bin Laden, rebuilding the country, and preparing for its first democratic elections. Only three years later, 8 million people voted during the historic election on October 9, 2004.[5] They elected Hamid Karzai as their first president.

Operation Iraqi Freedom

After Afghanistan, President Bush turned his sights on Saddam Hussein and his suspected weapons of mass destruction (WMDs) in Iraq. Since the end of the first Gulf War in

1991, numerous countries and the United Nations called for Saddam to disclose and disarm any WMDs. Saddam had used WMDs in the past. From 1987–88 his forces used poison gas on forty Kurdish villages, killing thousands of civilians. Saddam defied the United Nations (UN) and the world. On many occasions since 1991, he had kicked UN inspectors out of Iraq or did not provide them all the paperwork to show that he had disposed of his WMDs, as he claimed.

Saddam was given his last opportunity when the UN Security Council unanimously passed Resolution 1441 on November 8, 2002. Saddam again refused and the United States and some of its allies decided to attack Iraq, although a majority of UN countries did not approve.

Air Force stealth fighters dropped bombs on Iraqi leader Saddam Hussein's presidential palace compound during Operation Iraqi Freedom on March 21, 2003.

This is a US Air Force F117 stealth fighter, the kind of plane used to launch the first attacks against Iraq.

On March 17, 2003, President Bush gave Saddam and his sons forty-eight hours to leave Iraq or face a military conflict.[6] Operation Iraqi Freedom began on March 19, 2003. On the opening night of the campaign, the president was told that some "high-value" targets were meeting in a secret compound. President Bush ordered an attack on the location since he thought Saddam Hussein was there. With only two hours' notice, the Air Force sprang into action. Two F-117 stealth fighters dropped bombs on the compound in an effort to take out Saddam and quickly end the war. However, Saddam was not there.

Soon, hundreds of Air Force aircraft—from fighters and bombers to air refuelers, surveillance craft, and helicopters—joined forty-nine coalition countries, organized by President Bush, in taking out Saddam's command and control elements and military targets.

Air Force aircraft like the A-10 and MC-130 flew close air support missions to assist Marine and Army ground forces. By taking out tanks, artillery, radar, and reinforced locations, the Air Force helped to reduce the resistance US ground troops encountered.

Six weeks later, on May 1, 2003, the president said that while much dangerous work was still left to do, major combat operations in Iraq were over.

US Marines prepare to cross into Iraq from Kuwait, March 20, 2003. The US Air Force struck enemy targets to make the missions less dangerous for ground troops.

U.S. Airmen help clean out the Victory Over America Palace at Camp Slayer in Iraq. Saddam Hussein had begun building the palace after the 1991 Gulf War. The palace was turned over to Iraqi officials.

The Air Force controlled many of the remaining Iraqi airfields and airports, including Baghdad International Airport. Soon, numerous Air Force airplanes were flying in and out of the airport, bringing supplies to the frontline troops. To help ensure that America's largest cargo aircraft, the C-5 Galaxy, could come in with its 270,000-pound capacity loads, the Air Force sent reservists from Westover Air Reserve Base in Massachusetts to establish an air terminal operations center (ATOC). This ATOC served as a mobile air traffic control operation to ensure the mammoth plane could safely land in Baghdad.

CHAPTER 5

TODAY'S AIR FORCE

Following the breakup of the Soviet Union in 1989, and the end of the Gulf War in 1991, the administration of President George H.W. Bush began to reduce the size of the US military. The thinking at the time was to bring the military in line with diminished post-Cold War threats. Between 1992 and 2000, the Clinton Administration continued the reduction of forces, slashing national defense by more than half a million personnel and $50 billion in inflation-adjusted dollars. The number of total active personnel in the Air Force was decreased by nearly 30 percent. At the same time, the pace of deployments increased 16-fold after the end of the Cold War.

"This dramatic increase in the use of America's armed forces has had a detrimental effect on overall combat readiness," noted defense analyst Jack Spencer. "Both people and equipment wear out faster with frequent use. Frequent deployments also take funding away from ongoing expenses such as training, fuel, and supplies. Moreover, the stress of frequent and often unexpected deployments can be detrimental to troop morale and jeopardize the armed forces' ability to retain high-quality people."[1] Clearly, the Air Force needed a better way to manage its resources while retaining its battle readiness.

On August 4, 1998, then-Air Force secretary F. Whitten Peters and Air Force chief of staff General Michael Ryan announced that the Air Force would organize its combat and support assets into ten Aerospace Expeditionary Forces (AEFs).

Each of the AEFs would contain the Air Force weapon systems, people, and command and control needed to complete missions anywhere in the world. AEFs would be "on call" in pairs to respond to world events for a ninety-day period every fifteen months. For example, AEFs 1 and 2 would be on call to deploy if needed from January to March; AEFs 3 and 4 would be on call from April to June, and so on. This cycle would then be repeated every fifteen months. Air Force people and aircraft were assigned to one of the AEFs so they knew exactly when they would be on call to deploy.

The AEF concept became a reality in January 2000. While AEFs helped airmen deal with recurring deployments and small-scale "pop-up" crisis events, the AEF was not designed for fighting a major crisis. If war or a major crisis broke out, all resources would be used.[2] This occurred following the attacks on September 11, 2001, causing the Air Force to temporarily abandon the AEF concept.

The AEF concept resumed in July 2003. However, due to increased needs around the world, Air Force chief of

Air National Guard personnel make up a small percentage of the Air Force, but they fight alongside active duty Air Force personnel. Here, Air National Guardsmen arrive at Kandahar Airfield in Afghanistan in support of Operation Enduring Freedom.

staff General John Jumper extended AEF deployments to 120 days, up from the original 90 days. This meant airmen would be away from home one month longer. However, he also announced that the original fifteen-month rotation cycle would be extended to twenty months, so there was more time between deployments.[3]

Available Resources

Part of what made the AEF concept work was using all available resources, including the Air Force Reserve (AFR) and Air National Guard (ANG). In 2004, ANG and AFR airmen made up almost 14 percent of the total Air Force population. There were 107,000 ANG and 75,800 AFR troops compared to 359,000 active duty airmen.[4] When factoring in the aircraft and equipment, reserve forces make up about 45 percent of the total Air Force resources.

ANG and AFR airmen were fighting side-by-side with their active duty counterparts more than ever before and for longer periods of time. This meant there was a larger strain on reservists' civilian employers. Organizations such as the Employer Support for Guard and Reserve (ESGR), first organized in 1972, assist reservists and their civilian employers in dealing with the increased time away from the office. The Uniformed Services Employment and Reemployment Rights Act (USERRA) provides job protection to National Guard and Reserve members. It ensures that employers do not discriminate against reservists. USERRA also protects employers by ensuring they are notified of deployments and gives them a five-year limit to hold an employee's job.[5]

Today, the Air Force Reserve operates in various locations around the world. It has evolved from a "stand-by" force for emergencies into a Major Command (MAJCOM) of the active-duty Air Force. The Air Force Reserve currently performs about 20 percent of the work of the Air Force. Its operations include traditional flying missions and other more specialized missions, such as Weather Reconnaissance (Hurrican Hunters) and Aerial Fire Fighting and Personnel Recovery (Pararescuemen).[6]

Combat Air Patrols

The Air Force is the lead service for protecting US airspace through Operation Noble Eagle (ONE), using ten Air National Guard fighter wings in three air defense sectors around the nation. The Air Force ensures that the United States is protected from any possible aerial attack by flying combat air patrols over major US cities, and providing air support for major events such as presidential inaugurations and the Superbowl. From September 11, 2001, through March 2003, Air National Guard, Air Force Reserve, and active Air Force participating in ONE flew more than 27,625 fighter, tanker, and airborne early-warning missions.[7]

Kosovo Peacekeepers

Since June 1999, the Air Force, as part of the US European Command, has provided forces, aircraft, and logistical support to Operation Joint Guardian, the NATO-led peacekeeping operation in Kosovo. The NATO-led Kosovo Force (KFOR) includes forces from the United States, Great Britain, France, Germany, Italy, Czech Republic, Netherlands,

A US Air Force sergeant gives a care package filled with clothes, linens, hygiene items, and toys to a needy family in Gllogoc-Glogovac, Kosovo, during an international humanitarian mission.

An Air Force commander praises his airmen for their hard work and dedication.

Spain, Poland, Greece, Turkey, Russia, Canada, and Ukraine.[8] Today, this force is greatly reduced and its responsibilities have largely been transitioned to local Kosovo authorities.

7th Air Force

Since the end of the Korean War in the 1950s, the United States has remained in South Korea. Known as the 7th Air Force, this fighting unit is based at Osan Air Base in South Korea. It includes F-16s based at Kunsan Air Base in South Korea, and A-10s, F-16s, HH-60G helicopters, and U-2 reconnaissance aircraft also stationed at Osan. Some airmen stationed at Osan Air Base have the choice of doing a one-year tour by themselves or a two-year tour where they can bring their family if they are married or have children. Those selecting a one-year tour are allowed to come home for one month after the first six months away.

CHAPTER 6

AIR FORCE COMMANDS

The Department of the Air Force incorporates all elements of the Air Force. It is administered by a civilian Secretary and supervised by a military Chief of Staff. A Secretariat and an Air Staff help the Secretary and the Chief of Staff direct the Air Force mission. The Secretary of the Air Force reports to the Secretary of Defense, who in turn reports to the President of the United States. Contained within the Department of the Air Force are twelve major commands, six direct reporting units (DRUs), and twelve field operating units.

Each major command is made up of numbered air forces, which are made up of wings. A wing contains numerous groups, each of which is responsible for a function on a base, such as operations or medical. Groups are made up of squadrons and each squadron is made up of flights. Most wings have subunits located on a single Air Force base, although several have units located on multiple bases.

Major Commands (MAJCOMs)

Each of the Air Force's major commands, or MAJCOM, is responsible for a specific part of the Air Force, like training troops, fixing airplanes, or providing fighter and bomber forces.

Air Combat Command (ACC) Langley AFB

Air Combat Command is the largest MAJCOM and is headquartered at Langley Air Force Base in Virginia. ACC operates fighter, bomber, attack, reconnaissance, battle management, electronic-combat aircraft, and command-and-control systems. Some planes in ACC include the B-2 stealth fighter, the F-117 stealth fighter, and the F-22.

There are some one hundred thousand active duty airmen and more than ten thousand civilians assigned to ACC. In addition, more than fifty thousand Air National Guardsmen and more than ten thousand Air Force Reservists consider ACC their headquarters, bringing ACC's total to more than one hundred seventy thousand people.[1]

ACC has twenty-seven bases organized into four numbered air forces (1st Air Force, 8th Air Force, 9th Air Force, and 12th Air Force). ACC has three major subunits and a direct reporting unit called the Air and Space Expeditionary Force Center.

Air Education and Training Command (AETC) Randolph AFB

AETC is headquartered at Randolph Air Force Base in Texas and conducts recruiting, training, and education for all Air Force airmen such as basic military training, technical training, flying training, and professional military and degree-granting professional education.

AETC also operates basic military training for enlisted members; the US Air Force Academy, Reserve Officer Training Corps (ROTC), or Officer Training School (OTS) for officers; and flight training. Air University (AU) at Maxwell Air Force Base in Alabama is also part of AETC. AU is headquarters to the Air Force's programs for training officers like ROTC, Junior ROTC, and OTS; the Civil Air Patrol; officer and enlisted professional military education; and continuing education programs like the Air Force Institute of Technology, which is based at Wright-Patterson Air Force Base in Ohio.

There are more than seventy-six thousand active duty, ANG, AFR, civilians, and contract workers in AETC.[2]

Air Force Global Strike Command (AFGSC)
Barksdale AFB

Air Force Global Strike Command (AFGSC) is headquartered at Barksdale Air Force Base in the Shreveport-Bossier community of Louisiana. It is responsible for three intercontinental ballistic wings—the two B-52 wings, and the only B-2 wing. AFGSC provides combat-ready forces for nuclear deterrence and global strike operations.

Air Force Materiel Command (AFMC)
Wright-Patterson AFB

Air Force Materiel Command, based at Wright-Patterson Air Force Base, operates three major product centers that develop, acquire, test, and deploy air-delivered weapons, such as missiles and command-and-control systems used by commanders to fight wars. They also provide program management for everything from new weapons programs to retiring weapon systems.

Lackland Air Force Base in Texas offers a Summer Leadership program, where cadets can learn how to be military training instructors.

AFMC operates air logistics and test centers like the Aircraft Maintenance and Regeneration Center, Air Force Research Laboratory, Air Force Test Pilot School, and the Air Force School of Aerospace Medicine.

The command also runs the world-renowned Air Force Flight Test Center (AFFTC) at Edwards Air Force Base in California. The AFFTC provides aerospace research, development, test and evaluation, and support for the United States and its allies. It is commonly known as the home of the Air Force test pilot and was where Chuck Yeager broke the sound barrier in 1947.

Air Force Reserve Command (AFRC) Dobbins ARB

AFRC is headquartered at Dobbins Air Reserve Base in Georgia. Reservists, nicknamed "citizen airmen," perform nearly all the same functions as active duty airmen. There are more than one hundred twenty-five thousand airmen in AFRC in three numbered air forces (4th AF, 10th AF, and 22nd AF).[3] Westover Air Reserve Base, home to the 439th Airlift Wing and its massive C-5 Galaxy, is the Air Force's largest reserve base.

Most reservists are part-timers, meaning that they have regular civilian jobs and report to the base on one weekend per month for Unit Training Assembly and an additional fifteen annual tour days. Many are also Air Reserve Technicians (ARTs). ARTs are reservists who also work as military civilians during the week. Some have the same job during reserve weekends as they have during the workweek. The only difference is during the week they wear civilian clothes and do not follow normal military customs like saluting.

The Air Reserves provides airmen and aircraft usually during a national emergency. However, reservists also provide support in peacetime. It is divided into two sections: the Ready Reserve and the Standby Reserve. The Ready Reserve is called to fight in any emergency, while the Standby Reserve is called on in a time of war.

Air Force Space Command (AFSPC) Peterson AFB

AFSPC has one of the fastest-growing missions in the Air Force: the use and control of space for military purposes. Based at Peterson AFB in Colorado, AFSPC has four primary missions: space-force enhancement, space application, space support, and space control. More specifically, AFSPC

With its main landing gear not quite on the runway, the Space Shuttle *Endeavour* wraps up an eleven-day mission at Edwards Air Force Base, California.

operates the ballistic missile portion of the nation's nuclear-deterrent forces, places communications satellites into space, conducts counterspace operations like surveillance, and operates early-warning facilities around the country to protect from space-based attack.

Air Force Special Operations Command (AFSOC) United States and Japan

With fewer than twenty thousand airmen, AFSOC is the smallest MAJCOM and provides America's specialized air power.[4] This includes missions like information warfare, rescue operations, and specialized refueling. AFSOC also conducts psychological operations in which information is used against the enemy to destroy its morale or will to fight. In Iraq, for example, AFSOC units dropped leaflets over enemy territory to inform soldiers and civilians they were fighting Saddam Hussein and not the Iraqi people. The leaflets also let them know how to surrender. AFSOC operates out of three locations in the United States and Japan.

US Air Forces Central Command (USAFCENT) Shaw AFB

United States Air Forces Central Command (USAFCENT) is the air component of United States Central Command (USCENTCOM),a regional unified command. USAFCENT is responsible for air operations—either unilaterally or in concert with coalition partners. It is also charged with developing contingency plans in support of national objectives for USCENTCOM's 20-nation area of responsibility (AOR) in Southwest Asia. Additionally, USAFCENT manages an extensive supply and equipment prepositioning program at several AOR sites.

Air Mobility Command (AMC) Scott AFB

The massive planes that carry troops and equipment or refuel other aircraft are part of the Air Mobility Command. AMC manages air mobility during wartime by providing airlift, air refueling, special air missions, and medical-evacuation aircraft for US forces.

At nearly one hundred fifty thousand strong, AMC aircraft fly more than forty-one thousand hours per month, bringing supplies or troops to the front lines in places like Iraq.[5] They also conduct air refueling to ensure aircraft can accomplish their missions without having to land to refuel. AMC operates the Air Force's aeromedical evacuation aircraft that bring wounded and dead US service members back home. AMC is headquartered at Scott AFB in Illinois and has one numbered air force, 18th AF, also at Scott AFB.

Pacific Air Forces (PACAF) Hickham AFB

PACAF operates out of Hickam Air Force Base in Hawaii and is the oldest of Air Force MAJCOMs. Established in 1944, PACAF organizes, trains, equips, and maintains resources to conduct air operations throughout the Asia-Pacific region during peacetime, crisis, and war. There are more than fifty-four thousand airmen in PACAF at places like Japan, South Korea, Alaska, and Guam.[6]

United States Air Forces in Europe and Air Forces Africa (USAFE/AFAFRICA) Ramstein Air Base

US Air Forces in Europe and Air Forces Africa is the Air Force's other overseas MAJCOM. It is headquartered at Ramstein Air Base in Germany. Its area of responsibility spans 20.5 million square miles and ninety-three countries

The Air Force provided command and control, logistics, training and engineering support to the US government's efforts to contain the Ebola virus outbreak in West African nations in 2014.

from the northern tip of Greenland, to the eastern tip of Russia, to the southern tip of Africa. There are more than forty-two thousand airmen assigned to USAFE/AFAFRICA at bases in England, Germany, Turkey, Italy, Iceland, and the Azores, a small chain of islands off the coast of Portugal.[7]

Air National Guard (ANG)

When not called to active federal duty, Air National Guard (ANG) airmen are under the authority of the governors of the fifty states, Puerto Rico, Guam, the Virgin Islands, and the commanding general of the District of Columbia. Each governor is represented in the state or territory chain of command by an adjutant general. While ANG airmen train and prepare for war-related scenarios like the rest of the Air Force, governors can call them to preserve peace, order, and public safety. For example, they can provide assistance during emergencies, such as natural disasters and civil disturbances. ANG airmen conduct these missions because federal military troops are prohibited from conducting law enforcement activities in the United States. However, during wartime or threats to national security, the president has the authority to call up ANG airmen to active duty.

There are one hundred nine thousand ANG airmen playing a vital role in the overall Air Force mission. For example, the ANG provides 100 percent of the interceptor duties, 64 percent of the air-traffic control, 49 percent of the tactical airlift, 45 percent of the KC-135 refueling capability, 32 percent of the general-purpose fighter force, and 23 percent of the rescue-and-recovery capability.[8]

Direct Reporting Units

Direct reporting units (DRUs) are subdivisions of the Air Force, and report to Air Force headquarters at the Pentagon. They are separate from any MAJCOM because they have unique missions, legal requirements, or other factors. There are six DRUs: the Air Force District of Washington at Joint Base Andrews, Maryland, brings air, space, and cyberspace capabilities to the joint team protecting the nation's capital; the Air Force Network Integration Center at Scott Air Force Base, Illinois, provides cyber simulation/validation, and network standards, architecture, and engineering services; the Air Force Operational Test and Evaluation Center at various locations tests and evaluates space and warfighting systems; the Air Reserve Personnel Center at Buckley Air Force Base,

Colorado, is responsible for personnel support to nearly a million Air National Guard, Air Force Reserve, and retired members; the Arnold Air Force Base and Arnold Engineering Development Complex in Tullahoma, Tennessee, is the most advanced and largest complex of flight simulation test facilities in the world; and the Air Force Academy in Colorado Springs, Colorado, is a military academy for officer candidates for the United States Air Force.

Field Operating Agencies (FOAs)

The Air Force operates twelve Field Operating Agencies (FOAs), which are Air Force subdivisions carrying out activities under the control of a headquarters Air Force functional manager. One FOA is the Air Force Agency for Modeling and Simulation, based in Orlando, Florida. This agency develops new tactics and planning, and provides mission rehearsal and training. Another FOA is the Air Force Public Affairs Agency in San Antonio, Texas, which provides Airmen with unique public affairs resources to document and convey the Air Force mission and legacy.

CHAPTER 7

DIVERSITY IN THE AIR FORCE

The Air Force boasts a legacy of leading the way in removing barriers to opportunity. It considers diversity essential to remaining competitive in attracting, recruiting, and retaining America's best talent. Air Force diversity includes personal life experiences, geographic background, socioeconomic background, cultural knowledge, educational background, work background, language abilities, physical abilities, philosophical and spiritual perspectives, age, race, ethnicity, and gender. The Air Force values diversity and inclusivity and treats all its members with dignity and respect. As an all-volunteer force, it benefits immensely from the different perspectives and linguistic and cultural skills of all Americans.[1]

Women with Wings

While women in the past did play support roles during military conflicts, they did not have an active role in flight operations. As a result, the first hurdle women had to cross was proving they were fit to fly.[2] In the United States, Mary H. Myers set an altitude record in 1886 by soaring four miles above the earth in a balloon without oxygen equipment. American women, however, were initially barred from flying aircraft during World War I in England and the United States. In Europe, women were used as pilots almost from the beginning of the war. In Germany, women flew aircraft from factories to fields near the battlefronts. In Russia, women were given military ranks.[3] By the 1920s and 1930s, however, American women such as Amelia Earhart had captivated the country with their airborne feats.

Soon, Britain created a women's section of its Air Transport Auxiliary (ATA). Despite the fact that women faced discrimination, made less money than their male counterparts, and had to pay for their lodgings, the ATA flight records revealed that the accident rates for men and women were nearly identical.[4] During World War II, more than one hundred women were flying in the ATA.[5]

In 1941, pilot Jacqueline Cochran met Hap Arnold, a high-ranking Army Air Force officer, in Washington where he described the problem of ferrying bombers overseas. This job was being done by civilians since military pilots were needed for combat. Cochran suggested using women in this role. Arnold at first said he was not certain "whether a slip of a young girl could fight the controls of a B-17," but later agreed to allow Cochran to fly a bomber across the Atlantic on June 17, 1941.[6]

Arnold suggested Cochran fly with the ATA, and she brought a small group of women to Britain to train. To her surprise when she returned to America in 1942, she found out that Nancy Harkness Love was forming the Women's Auxiliary Ferrying Squadron (WAFS). Cochran organized a Women's Flying Training Detachment from a field in Houston to train pilots for eventual service in the WAFS. In May 1943, the group moved to Avenger Field in Sweetwater, Texas. The women lived in barracks under the same disciplinary rules as if they were actually in the military.[7]

On August 5, 1942, both groups merged, becoming the Women Airforce Service Pilots (WASP), led by Cochran.

Jacqueline Cochran led the Women Airforce Service Pilots (WASPs) during World War II.

WASPs leave their ship at the four engine school at Lockbourne. They were trained to ferry the B-17 Flying Fortresses.

WASPs began to ferry aircraft to bases around the United States and became involved in many kinds of flying except combat.

The WASP program ended when male military pilots began returning to the United States and resumed the ferrying role. Because of the success of the WASPs, Arnold was in favor of keeping the women pilots. However, without authorization to make them part of the military, he could not. During its time, WASP graduated 1,074 of its 1,830 recruits. The women delivered 12,650 planes of 77 different types while suffering only 38 deaths.[8]

Columbia Commander

Born on November 19, 1956, Colonel Eileen Collins became the first woman to command a Space Shuttle. Collins graduated in 1979 from Air Force Undergraduate Pilot Training and later became a C-141 pilot. She was selected for the astronaut program while attending the Air Force Test Pilot School. On July 23, 1999, she took the shuttle *Columbia* on a five-day mission to bring a powerful telescope to space to help study the universe.

She returned to space as commander of the shuttle Discovery on July 26, 2005. This was the first shuttle flight since the *Columbia* was destroyed while reentering Earth's atmosphere in February 2003. Her crew's mission was to test and evaluate new safety procedures put in place since the *Columbia* tragedy.[9]

Things began to change in 1948 when Congress passed the Women's Armed Forces Integration Act. Despite the fact the total air forces could not be made up of more than 2 percent by women and women could not be promoted above lieutenant colonel, women played a vital role in war. During the Korean War, Air Force nurses served as flight nurses in Korea. Many other servicewomen were assigned to duty in Japan and Okinawa.[10]

Public Law 90-130, which allowed the ANG to enlist women, was passed in 1968 and the first Air Force woman entered the ANG. A year later, the Air Force Reserve Officers Training Corps opened to women. In 1971, the first Air Force woman was promoted to brigadier general. In 1976, the Air Force Academy admitted the first female cadets and soon women began entering pilot training and Test Pilot School.

By the 1980s, women were involved in conflict, such as in Grenada during Operation Urgent Fury in 1983. In 1986, six Air Force women served as pilots, copilots, and boom operators on the KC-135 and KC-10 tankers that refueled FB-111s during the raid on Libya. That same year, the Air Force Academy's top graduate was a woman.

In 1989, 770 women participated in Operation Just Cause in Panama. Two earned the Air Medal with the "V" device that means they served in combat. During Operations Desert Shield and Desert Storm, over forty thousand Air Force women contributed to the missions. In 1991, Congress repealed the laws banning women from flying in combat.

In 1993, Dr. Sheila Widnall was the first woman to be named secretary of the Air Force and the first female service secretary in the history of the armed forces. During Operation Desert Fox in 1998, a woman was in the first wave of US strikes against Iraq. By 2004, women in the Air Force were fighting the war on terrorism throughout the world in many roles. To date, women in the Air Force are still restricted from becoming pararescue troops or combat controllers and from serving in those units and positions that routinely operate with direct ground combat units.[11]

Tuskegee Airmen Lead the Way

African Americans also experienced challenges to being fully accepted into the military. That began to change in 1941 with the passing of Executive Order 8802, which prohibited discrimination within the military.

Tuskegee Airmen stand with their fighter airplane at their flying school during World War II. They never lost an airman to enemy attacks.

On July 19, 1941, the Army Air Force began a program in Tuskegee, Alabama, to train black Americans as military pilots at the Tuskegee Institute. The first classes of Tuskegee Airmen were trained to be fighter pilots.

Thirteen started in the first class and five completed the training. One of them was Captain Benjamin O. Davis, Jr., who became the Air Force's first black general. Another famous Tuskegee Airman was Daniel "Chappie" James, Jr., who would later become the Air Force's first black four-star general.

The Tuskegee Airmen began overseas combat operations near Naples, Italy, in February 1944, flying air patrols over Naples Harbor and the Mediterranean Sea. In April 1944, the group transferred to the Adriatic Sea side of Italy near Foggia, and began conducting long-range heavy bomber escort missions for the 15th Strategic Air Force. In July 1944, the 99th Fighter Squadron was transferred to Ramitelli and the group became the only four-squadron fighter group performing bomber escort missions in the 15th Air Force.

In September 1943, a training program began at Tuskegee to develop bomber pilots. However, World War II ended before these men were able to get into combat. By the end of the war, 992 men had graduated from pilot training at Tuskegee, 450 of whom were sent overseas for combat assignment. During the same period, approximately 150 lost their lives while in training or on combat flights.

The Tuskegee Airmen earned significant recognition primarily because their squadron never lost a bomber to enemy attacks. They flew 15,000 combat sorties and destroyed 111 German airplanes in the air and 150 on the ground.[12]

African Americans would continue to play a large role in future conflicts. Two African Americans would go on to earn the Medal of Honor during World War II, two during the Korean War, and twenty in the Vietnam War.

Today, African Americans make up approximately 15 percent of the Air Force population. Many have attained the rank of four-star general. One was General Lloyd "Fig" Newton who was the commander of AETC and the first African American to be selected for the US Air Force Thunderbirds in 1974. This is a team of pilots that stages spectacular air demonstrations for the American public.

On May 15, 2005, African Americans in the Air Force reached another significant milestone when Colonel Stayce Harris became the first African-American woman to command a flying wing. She commanded the 459th Air Refueling Wing at Andrews Air Force Base in Maryland.

African Americans in the Air Force have also made their mark as astronauts. One was Lieutenant Colonel Michael P. Anderson who died on February 1, 2003, over the southern United States when space shuttle *Columbia* exploded and its crew perished during reentry. Anderson also flew aboard space shuttle *Endeavour* in January 1998.

Hispanic Pioneers

Hispanics have also made significant contributions to national defense and have earned more Medals of Honor than any other ethnic minority. Hispanics have been part of the defense of America since the Revolutionary War.

In 1929, Lieutenant General Elwood Quesada, a Hispanic, proved the importance of air refueling. He was a member of the famous "Question Mark" crew along with Major Carl Spaatz and others, which set a sustained in-flight refueling record of 151 hours—more than six days in the air over Los Angeles. Air refuelings take place when a tanker aircraft provides fuel to another aircraft in-flight using hoses or "booms." The plane flew eleven thousand miles and was air-refueled forty-three times; nine times were at night.[13]

Some five hundred thousand Hispanics served in the US armed forces during World War II. One, Oscar Perdomo, became the last ace of the conflict. Flying in a P-47N Thunderbolt near Okinawa on August 13, 1945, he encountered five Japanese aircraft and shot down three of them.

Oscar Perdomo was America's last "ace in a day" during World War II. He was awarded the Distinguished Service Cross and the Air Medal.

Later, he spotted two Japanese trainer aircraft and shot one down before being "jumped" by three more. In the ensuing combat, Perdomo achieved his fifth confirmed kill of the day. This Hispanic-American hero joined the most elite in the fighter community, an ace in a day.[14]

During the Korean War, US Air Force Captain Manuel J. Fernandez, an F-86 fighter pilot, was credited with over 14 enemy kills in 125 missions. He was the third-ranked fighter pilot of the war and retired as a colonel.

In Vietnam, Air Force Master Sergeant Juan J. Valdez climbed aboard the last US helicopter to depart the roof of the American Embassy in Saigon, ending the US presence in Vietnam, which spanned eighteen years. Valdez's presence confirmed the Latino theme of participation in America's wars: "First in . . . last to leave."[15] Approximately eighty thousand Hispanics served in the Vietnam War.

Hispanics also served valiantly during the Persian Gulf War and today continue to serve in leadership positions fighting the war on terrorism.

One current pioneer is Lieutenant Colonel Edward Cabrera, who in 2005 was commander of the 411th Flight Test Squadron at Edwards Air Force Base in California. Cabrera led an elite team of five of the best test pilots to gauge

Smilin' Sandy Sanchez

Technical Sergeant Sator "Sandy" Sanchez was a B-17 aerial gunner who volunteered to stay in combat even after reaching the required twenty-five combat missions. He flew a total of forty-four combat missions with the 95th Bomb Group. In recognition of his dedication, a B-17 was nicknamed *Smilin' Sandy Sanchez* in his honor. It is the only known B-17 aircraft ever named for an enlisted man. After a short rest in the United States, he volunteered for his third combat tour and was sent to the 15th Air Force in Italy. On March 15, 1945, he volunteered for his 66th and last mission. During the bombing run, his B-17 was hit and severely damaged. Everyone parachuted out of the plane except Sanchez. The B-17 exploded and crashed. Sanchez's body was never recovered.[16]

the war fighting abilities of the F/A 22 Raptor, the world's most advanced aircraft. As the United States' next generation air-dominance warplane, the Raptor has been given the role of maintaining and expanding the Air Force's superiority in the sky.

Down with "Don't Ask, Don't Tell"

Early in the 1992 presidential campaign, former President Bill Clinton promised that he would "lift the ban" on homosexuals serving in the military. The issue drew heated debate among policymakers and the public.

Some believed that homosexual conduct in the military represented an unacceptable risk to morale, good order and discipline, and unit cohesion—requirements that make military life different from civilian life. A policy was designed to balance both the unique demands of military life with the recognition that homosexuals have contributed to national defense. This policy was termed, "don't ask, don't tell," meaning service members would not be asked about their sexual orientation, as had previously been done on a form during enlistment in the Air Force. More specifically, the Department of Defense policy stated that sexual orientation is a personal and private matter and should not prohibit someone from serving in the military service, but open homosexual conduct would not be allowed.

The policy also stated that the armed services may not conduct an investigation to determine someone's sexual orientation. In 1980, prior to the policy, 1,754 people were forced to leave the military due to homosexual activity.[17] That number dropped to 770 in 2003.[18] The military policy toward homosexual conduct was upheld by many courts, including the US Supreme Court. On December 15, 2010, however, the House of Representatives voted to repeal "Don't Ask, Don't Tell" by passing bill H.R. 2965. Three days later, the Senate followed suit by passing bill S. 4023. President Barack Obama signed the repeal into law on December 22, 2010. The end of "Don't Ask, Don't Tell" was set at September 20, 2011.

Other Ethnic Groups

In addition to women, Hispanics, and African Americans, the Air Force and the federal government also formally recognize other minority groups during special observances. They include Asian-Pacific heritage month in May, Disability Employment Awareness Month in October, and American Indian and Alaska Native Heritage Month in November. Air Force airmen come from nearly all countries around the world. For example, in January 2006, there were 290 active-duty enlisted airmen who were born in Colombia, 25 from Cambodia, 38 from Ethiopia, four from Iraq, and one from Papua New Guinea. They join an organization that recognizes and celebrates their cultural and ethnic differences.[19]

AIR FORCE LIFE

The Air Force values its people and makes their well-being a top priority. It enjoys a reputation for providing the best quality-of-life programs of all the branches of military service. In advance of the other services, the Air Force used a substantial part of its funding to establish, maintain, or expand programs dedicated to providing its personnel with the highest possible standard of living.

Almost all Air Force bases resemble small US towns. For starters, most bases have a shopping area with a department store and other smaller shops. Operated by the Army and Air Force Exchange Service (AAFES), the Base Exchange or BX, offers tax-free shopping.

In addition, AAFES operates barbershops, fast food restaurants and flower shops. Other vendors like vitamin shops, Internet cafés, and coffee shops also operate here.

Most bases have restaurants; a grocery store, called the commissary; gas stations; and arts-and-crafts centers.

For entertainment, airmen can play golf on the base or watch a movie at the base movie theater. There are also bowling alleys and nightclubs on most bases. Since the Air Force promotes good physical conditioning, bases also offer gyms. Most have swimming pools and outdoor recreation facilities where airmen can rent boats and camping gear. Air Force bases also have facilities like schools, churches, and hospitals. Airmen living on base or near the base can have all the services they would normally find in a town.

Many airmen are also offered the opportunity to live on base. The only things airmen have to pay for are services like cable, telephone, and Internet access. Single enlisted members can stay in dorm-style rooms. Airmen with families are offered two- to four-bedroom houses on most bases.

Those who live off base are given a tax-free allowance to help pay for rent or a mortgage. The amount of the allowance is based on the airman's rank, the number of years in the Air Force, and location.

Additional Advantages

All Air Force airmen are given thirty days of vacation. When not in uniform, airmen can take advantage of travel opportunities offered on many military installations. For instance, airmen can hop a transport-type aircraft to many places around the world for free. Airmen and their families can fly to Hawaii from Travis Air Force Base in California, if there is space available on scheduled flights.

Those wishing to continue their education can sign up for college courses offered on base by different colleges and

An aerial view at McGuire Air Force Base in New Jersey shows the large scope of Air Force bases. In many ways, a base is like a small town.

universities. The Air Force even offers a tuition-assistance program to help pay for school. The program pays 100 percent (up to $250 per semester hour or equivalent) of the cost of college courses to a maximum of $4,500 per year.[1]

The Montgomery G.I. Bill is also available to provide assistance in paying for school and provides up to thirty-six months of benefits to those eligible. These benefits may be used for degree and certificate programs, flight training, apprenticeship or on-the-job training, and correspondence courses.

For enlisted members, the Air Force offers an associate's degree via the Community College of the Air Force. CCAF is

America's largest community college and is the only degree-granting institution in the world dedicated entirely to Air Force airmen.

For officers wishing to get a master's or other advanced degree directly related to their specialty, the Air Force offers its own fully-paid graduate school for engineering and management degrees called the Air Force Institute of Technology.

Active Involvement in the Community

Since bases are often near major towns and cities—not to mention the fact that the Air Force is funded through taxpayer dollars—the Air Force actively seeks ways to be

One resource available to Air Force members is continuing education. Here, airmen learn about leadership and the many resources available to help them have a successful Air Force career.

involved in the community and open its doors to its neighbors. Each base has a public affairs office that is responsible for maintaining the public's trust and support for the base, the Air Force, and the mission. One way Air Force public affairs offices do this is by inviting community groups on to the base for tours. In addition, most bases host airshows that often attract thousands of people to see aerial demonstrations and vintage aircraft and to converse with the Air Force men and women in uniform.

The US Air Force Thunderbirds perform for the public and educate young people about the Air Force.

A P-51 Mustang soars alongside an F-16 Fighting Falcon at the Warriors Over the Wasatch Air Show in Utah.

In addition to formal public affairs programs, Air Force airmen are actively involved in activities like Parent Teacher Associations, coaching, volunteering with churches and nonprofit organizations, as well as tutoring.

However, before anyone can do this as a United States airman, he or she must first take an important step. Joining the Air Force can be one of the biggest decisions in a young person's life.

DONNING THE AIR FORCE BLUE

The Air Force protects and defends America's freedoms in the air, space, and cyberspace. Joining the Air Force is a fairly simple process. Non-prior service applicants must be at least seventeen to apply and in basic military training before their fortieth birthday. Air Force recruiters are available in most cities and online to assist applicants and answer questions.

Enlisted Applicants

While it is possible to enlist with a general equivalency diploma (GED), generally one must be a high school graduate to join the Air Force. Recruits are given the Armed Services Vocational Aptitude Battery (ASVAB). The ASVAB is broken down into four categories: mechanical, administrative, general, and electronic. A overall score of 36 is the minimum qualifying score for a high school graduate and a 65 is required for someone with a GED. Each career field has minimum score requirements. The ASVAB scores, along with results from a physical examination are reviewed during job counseling in the enlistment process.

Once accepted, Air Force recruits are sent to a Military Entrance Processing Station, where they get a physical and eye exam, are weighed, and tested for drugs and diseases. Recruits are fingerprinted and interviewed by a counselor to help match the person's interest and ASVAB scores with the needs of the Air Force.

They are then sent to basic military training (BMT) at Lackland Air Force Base in Texas. The six-week course includes physical training, classroom instruction, field training, and instruction on Air Force customs.

From the minute trainees step off the bus, they are quickly prepared for the discipline they will need for the next six weeks and their entire Air Force career. They are assigned to a flight headed by a training instructor. When they first arrive, trainees are informally referred to as "rainbows" for the many colors they wear on their clothes and the color of their hair.

The first week is designed to provide many mental and physical challenges. Days begin at 5:00AM and include classroom instruction, physical conditioning, and training on customs like how to salute.

Physical conditioning is a major part of BMT. Trainees must pass two physical conditioning tests that consist of running, push-ups, and sit-ups in order to graduate. Males under 30 must run 1.5 miles in 11 minutes and 57 seconds and do at least 33 sit-ups and 42 push-ups. Women under 30 must run the 1.5 miles in 14 minutes and 26 seconds and do at least 38 sit-ups and 18 push-ups.[1]

Throughout the next few weeks, trainees are taught about the Air Force structure, ethics, and values. They participate in field training and run an obstacle course that builds confidence. They are also given training on shooting and cleaning the M16 rifle. Trainees can earn their first uniform ribbon by qualifying as an "expert" shooter.

In 1999, the Air Force introduced "Warrior Week" to prepare trainees for the reality of deployments they would likely face once on duty. Traditionally, the Air Force has not made a major effort to teach enlisted members soldiering

Trainees run the confidence course during Basic Military Training at Lackland Air Force Base in Texas.

skills. Since the Cold War ended, the Air Force has become smaller, but more airmen are being deployed to dangerous places. The Air Force estimates that 85 percent of all airmen entering service today will deploy to a world hot spot at least once during their career.

During Warrior Week, trainees learn how to build tents, put on chemical warfare protective equipment, and provide basic first aid. The whole exercise is built around an actual mission to defend the base from invasion by the enemy, a role played by the instructors.[2]

Following graduation, airmen are sent to technical training for the job, or specialty, they were assigned. Training is primarily conducted at Keesler AFB in Mississippi, or in Texas at Goodfellow AFB, Lackland AFB, or Sheppard AFB. For example, those entering computer-related fields normally go to Keesler AFB for training. Some specialized training can occur on the bases of other armed services, such as the Defense Information School at Fort Meade in Maryland for those entering the public affairs career field. Depending on the specialty, training can take a few weeks to a full year. Following this technical training, airmen are sent to their first duty station.

Generous Benefits

Enlisted airmen earn a salary based on rank and number of years in the Air Force. They are paid twice per month. Enlisted ranks go from airman basic (E-1) through chief master sergeant (E-9). For example, in 2015 an airman basic with four months in the Air Force earned a base salary of about $1,430 per month. A chief master sergeant with twenty-six years in the Air Force earned about $6,552 per month.

Fast Mover

Master Sergeant Stephanie D. Clark was part of the 88th Aerial Port Squadron at McGuire AFB, New Jersey, when she was sent to support Operation Iraqi Freedom. She first went to Charleston AFB in South Carolina, where she led her section to an all-time record of moving more than 11,278 tons in 24 days aboard four types of aircraft bound for the war on terrorism. Three months later, she became the passenger service supervisor at Baghdad International Airport. Her work in moving 17,800 passengers got her selected as the noncommissioned officer in charge. She was responsible for all aspects of air logistics operations. After demobilization, coalition officials asked her to return to Iraq to instruct Iraqi police on techniques in counterterrorism and special operations.

However, basic pay is only one part of the pay equation. The Air Force pays bonuses for many career fields where there are shortages of people or the jobs are very stressful. Single enlisted airmen are also provided free room and board and a clothing allowance; some earn hazardous-duty or foreign-language pay. Married airmen living off base are provided money for food and housing. These allowances are tax free. Airmen also have a generous retirement plan where they can retire with up to 50 percent of their final base salary after twenty years of active duty service. The Air Force also provides $500,000 in life insurance benefits for less than $30 per month.

After factoring in the free medical and dental benefits, a gym, tax-free shopping, educational benefits, and recreation programs, some consider the total compensation package in the Air Force very attractive and competitive with other career choices.

Airmen also have an opportunity to be promoted to higher ranks. Each year, airmen are evaluated by their supervisors in an Enlisted Performance Review. Promotions are also based, in part, on awards and decorations. Medals include the Defense Service Medal and the Medal of Honor, and the more common Good Conduct Medal, Achievement Medal, and Meritorious Service Medal. Many who have performed with honor while in direct contact with the enemy have earned the Bronze Star. Those hurt or killed in action are awarded the Purple Heart.

Commissioned Officer

A commissioned officer in the Air Force must have at least a four-year college degree. Officers fill unit command and operational career fields such as pilots; navigators; and battle management managerial, professional, and technical jobs. Officers take the Air Force Officer Qualifying Test (AFOQT), a test similar to the SAT. The AFOQT is used to select applicants for officer commissioning programs, such as the Air Force Academy, Officer Training School (OTS) or Air Force Reserve Officer Training Corps (ROTC). It is also used for selection into specific training programs such as pilot and navigator training.

The AFOQT can generally only be taken twice and candidates must wait 180 days between tests. Certain career fields have minimum scores. For example, to be a pilot you must score a 25 on the pilot section, which measures knowledge of aviation and mechanical systems, the ability to read aircraft instruments, and other flight-related knowledge.

United States Air Force Academy (USAFA)

Located in Colorado Springs, Colorado, the USAFA is one of the nation's premier undergraduate institutions. Cadets complete four years of studies and earn a bachelor of science degree. Emphasis is placed on academics, military training, athletic conditioning, and spiritual and ethical development.

Academics include classes in science, engineering, social sciences, and military studies. Cadets can specialize in more than thirty majors. USAFA has twenty-nine men's and women's intercollegiate sports teams that compete nationally. The physical education program consists of mandatory courses and electives ranging from judo to SCUBA.

The Honor Code is the centerpiece of a cadet's moral and ethical development. Cadets pledge: "We will not lie, steal, or cheat, nor tolerate among us anyone who does." All cadets take formal courses and instruction on honor and ethics.[3]

Following graduation, cadets are commissioned as second lieutenants. Most must make a five-year commitment to the active duty Air Force. Pilots must make a ten-year commitment.

The USAFA is selective, and the process of getting accepted starts early with good grades, extracurricular activities, and good leadership traits. About 85 percent of USAFA cadets finished in the top quarter of their high school class, and 11 percent graduated first in their class.

Cadets at the Air Force Academy in Colorado Springs, Colorado, earn a four-year bachelor of science degree.

The average cadet scored a 1296 on the two-part SAT. On the ACT, the cadet mean for English is 30 for both reading and mathematics. Candidates should meet with their guidance counselor to schedule the Preliminary Scholastic Aptitude Test (PSAT) as a sophomore in high school and should take the SAT or ACT during their junior year.[4]

Candidates must also meet with an Air Force Academy Admissions Liaison Officer (ALO) or an Academy representative. During an interview with one of them, you may ask any questions you have about the Academy and speak directly with the people who will review your record. Guidance counselors have the names of local ALOs.

Finally, to increase the chances of being selected, candidates should obtain a nomination from their US representative, one of their US senators, or the vice president. Each member of Congress and the vice president may have five nominated cadets at the Air Force Academy at any one time. They may nominate up to ten candidates for each vacancy. Vacancies occur when cadets graduate or leave prior to graduation. The academy also reserves a select number of spots for international applicants and applicants from US territories and military-affiliated categories.

Reserve Officers Training Corps (ROTC)

Air Force Reserve Officer Training Corps (ROTC) is open to full-time students at more than 1,100 colleges and universities in the continental United States, Puerto Rico, and Hawaii. A host university is a college or university that offers an Air Force ROTC program to its students right there on campus. A crosstown university is a college or university that offers Air Force ROTC, but whose students take their AFROTC classes each week at the nearest host university.

ROTC is the largest supplier of officers to the armed forces.[5] Credit for a portion of the first year of the four-year program may be provided for completion of at least two years of junior ROTC, a high school version of the program, participation in the Civil Air Patrol, military school training, or prior US military service.

More than sixty-five hundred scholarships are available and pay for either full or partial tuition, books, laboratory fees, and extra spending money that increases each year in the program. While scholarships are available for any degree program, those with scientific and technical-related majors have priority.[6] The deadline to apply for a scholarship is December 1 for high school seniors.

An Air Force ROTC student experiences what it is like to free fall in a parachute by hanging in a parachute rig during a training session.

Those already in college can also join ROTC if they have at least a 2.5 GPA and are a US citizen by the time they would graduate. They must also pass the AFOQT and a physical fitness test and meet the ROTC weight and body fat standards. They must also pass a physical examination and review board.

Finally, cadets cannot be conscientious objectors, who would not participate in war or take up arms because of religious training or beliefs.

Once accepted, cadets who are underclassmen (freshmen and sophomores) enter the General Military Course (GMC), which covers the development of airpower and Air Force structure. Students take courses in Aerospace Studies. AS100 is the student's first introduction to the Air Force. The AS200 course focuses on the history of airpower and how politics can affect the use of military power.

Upperclassmen enter the Professional Officer Course (POC), which covers Air Force leadership and management, as well as US defense policy. AS300 discusses the skills needed to be a successful leader and manager. Case studies on leadership are discussed and cadets are given problem-solving exercises. AS400 examines national security, methods of managing conflict, alliances and regional security agreements, and analysis of the threats of war.

In addition to academic classes, both GMC and POC cadets participate in Leadership Laboratory. Called "Lead Lab" for short, it provides cadets with an opportunity to develop leadership skills and apply what they learned in the classroom. Cadets are introduced to Air Force customs, courtesies, drills, and ceremonies like marching and how to properly wear the uniform. Cadets often take field trips to Air Force bases or have Air Force officers speak to them about their careers and experiences.[7]

During the summer between the sophomore and junior year, cadets are sent to field training, the ROTC version of BMT. This is a four- or six-week course that exposes cadets to military life and teaches them about leadership. This intensive course challenges cadets mentally and physically. After successful completion of field training, cadets return to campus and sign an Air Force contract to continue in the program. Cadets can take ROTC for two years and go through field training before they have to formally sign a contract and make a commitment to the Air Force.

After graduation, cadets are commissioned as second lieutenants in the Air Force and usually enter one of the career choices they have indicated they would like to fill. Those selected as pilots must serve ten years after completing a 49-week flight training course. Navigators must serve five years after navigator training plus a two-year inactive reserve commitment. Nonflying officers serve four years of active duty with a four-year inactive reserve commitment.

Officer Training School (OTS)

The third primary way to be commissioned an officer in the US Air Force is through the Officer Training School at Maxwell AFB in Alabama. OTS has the mission of "Building today's leaders for tomorrow's Air Force."

OTS provides a twelve-week basic officer training (BOT) course programmed to train and commission one thousand officers annually. Additionally, OTS conducts a four-week commissioned officer training (COT) program to teach leadership skills to more than fifteen hundred new judge advocates, chaplains, and medical officers each year. Officer Training School is for those with the talent and drive to become a leader in the Air Force.[8]

Commissioned Compensations

Because of their added responsibility and accountability, officers are compensated more than enlisted members. This is not to say enlisted members are less important.

Officer rank goes from second lieutenant to general. Each rank has an associated pay grade. For example, a second lieutenant is an O-1, a first lieutenant an O-2, and so on all the way to general, an O-10. There are four different types of generals. A brigadier general has one star, a major general two stars, a lieutenant general three stars, and a general has four stars on his or her uniform.

Officers in careers such as pilots, navigators, and doctors receive extra special duty pay to help ensure their pay is similar to their civilian counterparts. Otherwise, it would be difficult to recruit officers in these careers that pay high salaries in the civilian world.

Similar to enlisted members, officers have a retirement plan; are provided hazardous-duty pay if warranted; get life insurance, medical and dental coverage; and receive other benefits, such as travel and thirty days of vacation time.

Challenges and Risks

While the benefits and pay are appealing, the Air Force is not without its challenges and risks. Many recruits do not make it through basic training for reasons both physical and mental. In addition, the Air Force is focused on mobility, meaning the ability to move its forces and people to areas around the world. As a result, most airmen will at one point or another find themselves in direct support of an overseas conflict. In the past, pilots were most at risk of being killed by the enemy in combat. Today, the Air Force is playing a more operational role. This means people who are not pilots are also being sent to the frontlines. So, anyone who joins the Air Force could be deployed to an area where airmen are in danger of being killed or injured.

Once one has weighed the risks and rewards and has decided to join the Air Force, there are a number of career opportunities that await.

AIR FORCE CAREER CHOICES

Though the Air Force is known for its expertise in aviation, pilots make up only slightly more than 4 percent of its staffing. Many career opportunities are available to enlisted applicants and officer candidates. Airmen can choose from more than 130 career specialties, while officers can select from forty-seven primary career choices. It takes a lot of support people to "keep 'em flying."

Enlisted Career Paths

Enlisted opportunities fall into one of four main career paths: mechanical, administrative, general, and electronics.

Mechanical

The Air Force develops and operates some of the most sophisticated and complicated equipment and is in need of those with the mechanical skills to run them. Airmen in a mechanical career field could be working as an aircraft mechanic or with radio systems, munitions, or vehicles.

Aircraft mechanics, for example, do everything from repairing engines to inspecting and operating ejection seats. Aircraft mechanics are the backbone of the flying operation and are a major reason the planes get off the ground. Mechanics work in crews and are usually assigned to a particular type of airplane, which they get to know better than their own automobiles.

There are also unique opportunities in this career area such as being an aerial gunner on an airplane or helicopter. Aerial gunners perform missions like operating a weapon system on a helicopter while looking for a downed pilot. They are placed on flying status as an aircrew member, which means they earn more through flight and hazardous duty pay.

Another unique job is a missile and space systems maintenance apprentice, who maintains, assembles, and inspects the Intercontinental Ballistic Missiles (ICBMs). ICBMs are always on alert to respond against enemies thousands of miles away. However, they are only effective if they are well maintained.

Administrative

Administrative careers cover the many day-to-day base operations such as food, equipment, and housing that are critical to Air Force operations.

One career is airfield management, which plays a major role in a pilot's ability to land, take off, and taxi on runways and taxiways throughout the world. Airfield managers inspect airfields worldwide, monitor airfield construction projects, and issue notices to airmen for flight hazards or restrictions

An Air Force aircraft mechanic works on a B-52 Stratofortress aircraft engine.

Bomb Disposal

Staff Sergeant Aaron D. Davenport, an Explosive Ordnance Disposal equipment technician, deployed to Iraq six months after returning from duty in Afghanistan. He earned an Air Force Achievement Medal for his actions during covert recovery of a downed C-130 aircraft. He destroyed twelve 120 mm mortar tubes in hidden weapons caches. His role in eliminating from a playground seventy-seven bomblets, which are small bombs dropped from a larger bomb, ensured the safety of five hundred Iraqi children. Working with the US Army, he helped dispose of more than eighty-three thousand Iraqi munitions. He was a key player in support of a Marine Corps raid on an Iraqi surface-to-air missile battery, re-sulting in the destruction of seven SA-7 missiles. He also helped remove weapons caches endangering two thousand coalition forces in Saudi Arabia.

at the airfield or in the airspace that would pose flight-safety problems. If the airfield managers say something is not safe, all flying stops.

General

The Air Force offers seventy-two types of general careers that are less mechanical in nature. These can include working in air traffic control, speaking foreign languages as a linguist, or collecting and analyzing intelligence.

General careers can also be in the medical field where airmen could work at a laboratory, in a clinic or pharmacy, or as medical-support persons inside an emergency room or in a war zone helping to treat wounded airmen. For example, an aeromedical apprentice assists in the care of patients during emergency medical flights as an airborne emergency medical technician (EMT). An aeromedical apprentice works closely with the flight surgeon to ensure that pilots and navigators, missile alert crewmembers, and air traffic control airmen are ready for duty. They also assist in minor surgical procedures.

While an aerial gunner would help protect the aircraft and a downed pilot during a combat search and rescue mission, it is the job of the pararescue apprentice to physically rescue a downed aircrew member. Pararescuemen also provide specialized aerospace rescue and recovery support for NASA's space shuttle flights. They are certified scuba divers and skilled in surface water operations—both scuba and amphibious, and are trained as combat medics. This is one of the few career fields open only to men.

Electronics

As electronics become smaller and more powerful, they are increasingly used in Air Force weapon systems. Airmen in an electronics career field are trained to work with radar, avionics systems, surveillance systems, and missile and space systems.

After training at either Lackland AFB or Sheppard AFB in Texas, a bomber avionics systems instrument and flight control apprentice would perform operational checks and fix malfunctions of flight control systems on either the B-2 stealth bomber or the B-1. He or she is responsible for several of the advanced bomber's aircraft systems, including the automatic pilot, flight controls, navigation, and hydraulic system indicators.

An Air Force aerial reconnaissance weather officer points to the eye of a storm during a hurricane flight off the coast of Hawaii.

Weather plays a significant role in successful military operations. Without accurate weather predictions, missions could be jeopardized because planes might not take off or land safely or targets might not be visible to nonradar or satellite-guided munitions. A weather apprentice analyzes and forecasts weather and space conditions for military decision-makers. Air Force weather apprentices receive training to understand the Earth's atmosphere and how to predict changes using satellite, radar, and computers.

Officer Specialties

Officers also have a wide variety of specialties from which to choose. They typically fall into four career paths: flight, nontechnical, specialty, and technical.

Flight

Without flying there would be no Air Force. Air crews, however, are not just pilots. There are opportunities as a navigator, air battle-manager, radar navigator, and weapons navigator.

Pilots or navigators could be flying in a fighter, reconnaissance, surveillance, bomber, or airlift aircraft. However, aviation careers do not stop at the edge of the atmosphere. Officers can also compete to enter the astronaut program.

Those selected as pilot candidates attend the fifty-two week Joint Specialized Undergraduate Pilot Training (JSUPT). Civilian flight instructors conduct this training in aircraft such as the Cessna 152. Students receive fifty hours of instruction and must qualify for a private pilot certificate.

The JSUPT program is conducted with the Navy at Vance AFB in Oklahoma and Naval Air Station Whiting Field in Florida. Students complete primary flight training in the Air Force's T-37B and the Navy's T-34. Other students complete the primary training at Columbus AFB in Mississippi, or Laughlin AFB in Texas, flying the T-37B.

After the first part of JSUPT, students move on to advanced training. Students selected for fighter-bomber planes train in the T-38A. Those selected as airlift-tanker pilots complete their training in the T-1A at Columbus AFB in Mississippi, Laughlin AFB in Texas, or Vance AFB

After fourteen virtual training missions in a flight simulator, the first female F-35 pilot prepares to take flight in the F-35A Lightning II joint strike fighter.

in Oklahoma, where they learn about air-to-air refueling, airdrop missions, and navigation.

Students selected to fly the C-130 Hercules train in the T-44 turboprop trainer at Naval Air Station Corpus Christi in Texas. Other students are selected to fly helicopters and complete their training at Fort Rucker in Alabama, in the UH-1 Huey. Helicopter training includes skills such as low-level flying.[1]

Nontechnical

These nontechnical positions require people who can take charge and demonstrate leadership. Opportunities are available in areas such as intelligence, personnel, security forces, and communications. There are also opportunities as a space operations officer controlling one of the Air Force's multibillion-dollar space systems or helping to launch a wide range of satellites into orbit.

One unit, the 7th Space Warning Squadron at Beale AFB in California, works inside a ten-story, pyramid-like structure that itself is a radar system called Precision Acquisition of Vehicle Entry Phased Array Warning System (PAVE PAWS). It is a fancy way of saying that they continuously scan the horizon to detect and track sea-launched ballistic missiles (SLBMs) and intercontinental ballistic missiles (ICBMs) headed toward North America.

Fortunately, there have been no enemy missiles for them to track, so the men and women of PAVE PAWS have another mission: to provide space surveillance and track objects in Earth's orbit. Their data is used to create a satellite catalog database that includes more than twenty-seven thousand

An operations officer schedules training flights.

man-made objects in orbit. About nine thousand of them require careful watching so they do not collide with satellites or space shuttles.[2]

Specialties

These careers are highly specialized jobs that require specific skills such as judge advocates, special investigative officers, and band officers.

This career path also includes base chaplains who provide religious support to Air Force airmen. Chaplains develop and administer chaplain service policies; provide professional religious support; and advise commanders on religious, ethical, moral, morale, and quality-of-life issues. Chaplains also offer ministry to the many religious beliefs found in a military community. Active duty and Reserve chaplains are responsible for supporting the free exercise of religion for all airmen, their dependents, and other people authorized on base.

Technical

While not many specialties fall under this category, technical careers are critical to the mission success of the Air Force. These careers include acquisition manager, aerospace engineer, mechanical engineer, scientist, and weather officer.

One specialty that has become increasingly important in the Air Force is the civil engineer. Often, the Air Force enters an area overseas without any infrastructure, which the Air Force refers to as a "bare base" location. Civil engineers build and maintain the buildings and utilities to operate a new location and specialize in areas including architectural, electrical, mechanical, and environmental engineering. They

An explosive ordnance disposal technician performs an inspection on a remote operated neutralization system used to retrieve explosive devices.

turn the bare base into a hustling-and-bustling installation complete with sleeping quarters; command-and-control buildings; functioning runways; and working water, power, and other utilities. Civil engineers also dispose of conventional, nuclear, and chemical weapons.

Many civil engineers, both officer and enlisted, attend the Air Force Combat Ammunition Center (AFCOMAC) training program, commonly referred to as "Ammo University." Located at Beale AFB in California, this course was developed to provide advanced training in combat ammunition planning and production.[3]

BEYOND THE WILD BLUE HORIZON

"The American people expect our Air Force to fly, fight, and win against any adversary," said Secretary of the Air Force Deborah Lee James, at a "State of the Air Force" press conference on January 15, 2015, in Washington, D.C. "It is important that we continue to afford our nation the Air Force capability it needs well into the future by appropriately investing in our people and our platforms."[1] To maintain its strategic advantage in an increasingly dangerous world, the Air Force must continue to adapt and respond faster than its potential adversaries, while operating with reduced forces and diminishing budgets. Therewith lies the Air Force's greatest challenge for the next three decades.

Today, there are no military forces around the world that can take on the Air Force in direct combat. This means that future wars will continue to be smaller in scale than the two world wars. Enemies around the globe will continue to fight the United States using terrorism or attacking with unconventional weapons, such as computer viruses or chemical and biological weapons. As a result, the Air Force must be a responsive force and remains committed to the Air Expeditionary Force (AEF) concept. There are about thirty thousand airmen deployed all around the world as part of an AEF.[2]

In addition, the Air Force continues to include space operations in military planning. The Air Force has taken the lead in making space the new battlefront. Space systems were an integral part of Operation Enduring Freedom and Operation Iraqi Freedom. For example, airmen used satellite feeds to identify and strike the broadcast capabilities of Iraqi state-run television. This space-based information was sent to Predator unmanned aerial vehicles that then fired Hellfire missiles in an effort to destroy the key source of Saddam Hussein's propaganda.[3]

One newer unit is the 527th Space Aggressor Squadron based at Schriever Air Force Base in Colorado. The unit was activated in October 2000 to realistically play "the bad guys" during training exercises that teach space operators ways to defend space capabilities such as communications, surveillance, and navigation systems from enemy attack.[4]

Protecting information and communications systems will also be an area of increasing importance for the Air Force. Because the Air Force relies on computers and networks for nearly all of its functions, they are an area of possible enemy attack. Viruses, deception, and illusions are some ways enemies could conduct information warfare.

There is no match for the US Air Force around the world. Here, three F-5E Tiger II aircraft fly in formation.

The Air Force continues to develop newer aircraft, weapon systems, and technologies to give airmen the edge in combat. Some, like unmanned aerial vehicles (UAV), help airmen avoid flying into highly defended enemy airspace altogether. A UAV is a drone that is piloted by remote control or through programs in its computer system.

One UAV, called Predator, is used to conduct reconnaissance over hostile territory. It is equipped with cameras that can transmit live footage of enemy actions to a commander on the ground or a fighter aircraft overhead. This information allows commanders to take out targets faster than ever before.

Because of their success in places like Kosovo, the Air Force began adding lasers on UAVs to "paint," or identify, a target. A laser-guided bomb delivered from an aircraft like the F-117 stealth fighter could then follow the laser beam and take out the target with incredible accuracy.

In the late 1990s, the Air Force began testing UAVs armed with Hellfire missiles in combat in Iraq. The results were mixed. The Predator performed well but the Hellfire missile was not a big enough weapon to take out large targets. However, this test encouraged the Air Force to continue to develop armed UAVs.

Another UAV called RQ-4 Global Hawk made its debut during the war in Afghanistan in 2002. It flies at altitudes above sixty thousand feet and will likely replace the U-2 Dragonlady. It does not shoot live video like the Predator but can capture images at night or through bad weather. It can fly for nearly a day and a half without refueling and can beam its images in real time to battlefield commanders or other platforms.[5] The Air Force is also developing a bomber version of a UAV called a UCAV (unmanned combat air vehicle).

In addition, after years of development, the F-22 is now streaking across the sky in combat. After years of testing, the F-22 was declared ready for war in December 2005, and were based initially at Langley AFB in Virginia, home to the famed 1st Fighter Wing. The F-22 replaced the F-15 as the premier air-to-air fighter.

Another emerging weapon system is the YAL-1A airborne laser aircraft, which is a 747 aircraft that carries a laser designed to shoot down ballistic missiles in their take-off phase, when they are still over enemy territory. The megawatt-class chemical oxygen iodine laser (COIL) produces a beam powerful enough to burn a small hole in the missile.

The F-22 Raptor was designed for both air and ground combat and electronic warfare. The Raptor is a stealth aircraft developed for the Air Force.

Because a missile uses extreme pressure during take-off, a slight hole in the missile would result in an explosion.

These technological advancements are designed to be used with other services since the Air Force is only one branch of the US military. Training exercises such as the Combined Joint Training Force Exercise (CJTFEX), run out of Langley AFB, put the other US military elements together with forces from the United Kingdom, Canada, the Netherlands, Norway, France, Germany, and Peru to train using realistic scenarios.

However, the Air Force recognizes that no weapon, system, or aircraft is sophisticated enough to operate without people. As a result, taking care of airmen continues to be the Air Force's top priority. Airmen carry out the mission and ensure the success and future of the US Air Force.

The Air Force is looking at the factors that affect recruiting and retention to ensure the right people enter the Air Force and the right people remain. Many career fields are highly stressed, meaning they have few people filling positions that are in high demand. The Air Force will add more people to these career fields through recruiting and retraining airmen from other career fields.

In January 2015, at the "State of the Air Force" press conference, Air Force Chief of Staff General Mark A. Welsh III spoke of the future of the Air Force:

> *Our vision [is] who we would like to be some day. It's something that just keeps calling us forward. Global reach, global vigilance, and global power—It's what we do for America. A Call to the Future—the lead document in our strategic document series—this is who we are going to be 20 years from now. New Air Force Concept of Operations [is] how we're going to operate once we get to that point. It gives us a target. It gives us a concept of how capabilities will fit together. The new Single Air Force Master Plan [is] the game plan to make the Call to the Future and Concept of Operations a reality.*[6]

General Welsh and Secretary of the Air Force Deborah Lee James are working hard to find a balance and refocus the Air Force to ensure that it remains the best in the world far into the future.

APPENDIX

Enlisted Pay Chart

Enlisted			
Pay Grade	Rank	Approximate Salary*	Insignia
E-1	Airman Basic	under 4 months: $1,430 per month; over 4 months: $1,546.80 per month	No insignia
E-2	Airman	$1,734.00 per month	
E-3	Airman First Class	$1,823.40–2,055.30 per month**	
E-4	Senior Airman	$2,019.60–2,451.60 per month	
E-5	Staff Sergeant	$2,202.90–3,125.70 per month	
E-6	Technical Sergeant	$2,404.50–3,724.20 per month	
E-7	Master Sergeant***	$2,780.10–4,996.20 per month	
E-8	Senior Master Sergeant***	$3,999.00–5,703.60 per month	
E-9	Chief Master Sergeant***	$4,885.20–7,584.60 per month	

* Approximate salaries are as of 2015 and do not include food and housing allowances, free healthcare, money for college, and bonuses.
** Salary for ranks E-3 through E-9 depend on the number of years in service.
*** A diamond in the insignia denotes First Sergeant status as well.

Officer Pay Chart

Enlisted			
Pay Grade	Rank	Approximate Salary per month*	Insignia
O-1	Second Lieutenant	$2,934.30–3,692.10	
O-2	First Lieutenant	$3,380.70–4,678.50	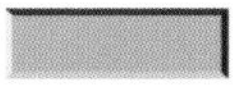
O-3	Captain	$3,912.60–6,365.40	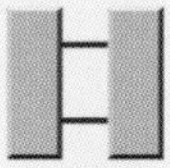
O-4	Major	$4,449.90–7,430.10	
O-5	Lieutenant Colonel	$5,157.60–8,762.40	
O-6	Colonel	$6,186.60–10,952.40	
O-7	Brigadier General	$8,264.40–12,347.70	
O-8	Major General	$9,946.20–14,338.50	
O-9	Lieutenant General	$14,056.80–17,436.90	
O-10	General	$16,072.20–19,762.50	

* Salaries are as of 2015 and do not include food and housing allowances, free healthcare, money for college, and bonuses; also, an approximate salary range has been given for each rank.

Air Force Awards

Enlisted		
Name	**Description**	**Medal**
Afghanistan Campaign Medal	For serving in Afghanistan on or after October 24, 2001	
Air Force Cross	For extraordinary heroism, not justifying the Medal of Honor	
Airmen's Medal	For heroism, usually where one risks his or her life, not involving actual combat	
Bronze Star	For heroic service not involving aerial flight	
Defense Distinguished Service Medal	Awarded to high-ranking military officers	
Distinguished Flying Cross	For heroism while participating in aerial flight	
Distinguished Service Medal	For exceptional service	
Global War on Terrorism Service Medal	For serving in the Global War on Terrorism	
Iraq Campaign Medal	For serving in Operation Iraqi Freedom	
Medal of Honor	The highest honor someone serving in the military can receive	
Purple Heart	For being injured or killed in the line of duty	
Silver Star	For brave action against the enemy	

TIMELINE

December 17, 1903—The Wright Brothers make the first powered airplane flight.

June 20, 1941—Creation of the Army Air Force (AAF) headed by Major General H.H. Arnold.

July 19, 1941—AAF begins program in Tuskegee, Alabama, to train African Americans as military pilots.

December 1, 1941—Creation of the Civil Air Patrol (CAP).

December 7, 1941—Japanese attack on Pearl Harbor in Hawaii.

December 8, 1941—US declares war on Japan.

April 18, 1942—America strikes back at Japan during the "Doolittle Raid."

August 17, 1942—The 97th Bomb Group makes first US heavy bomber raid in Europe when twelve B-17s attack a railroad yard in France.

August 4, 1943—Women Airforce Service Pilots (WASP) formed with Jacqueline Cochran as director.

June 6, 1944—With support from the AAF, US troops storm Normandy, France, on "D-Day."

May 8, 1945—The Nazis are defeated and the war in Europe ends, on "V-E day."

August 6, 1945—A B-29, the *Enola Gay,* drops an atomic bomb over Hiroshima.

August 9, 1945—Another B-29, *Bockscar,* drops a second atomic bomb over Nagasaki.

August 15, 1945—Japan surrenders.

September 18, 1947—The Air Force becomes its own service.

October 14, 1947—Chuck Yeager becomes first man to fly faster than the speed of sound.

June 26, 1948—Operation Vittles, the first mission of the Berlin Airlift, begins.

July 1, 1949—Segregation in the Air Force ends.

June 25, 1950—Thousands of North Koreans storm South Korea starting the Korean War.

May 29, 1952—First Air Force combat use of air-to-air refueling.

July 27, 1953—Korean War ends.

October 14, 1962—Two Air Force U-2s take photographs of Soviet missile construction in Cuba.

February 8, 1965—The Air Force conducts its first retaliatory air strike in North Vietnam.

March 2, 1965—The Air Force begins Operation Rolling Thunder bombing campaign against North Vietnam.

March 17, 1971—Jane Leslie Holley becomes the first woman commissioned through the Air Force Reserve Officer Training Corps program.

May 10, 1972—Operation Linebacker begins during the Vietnam War.

April 29, 1975—American involvement in South Vietnam ends.

September 1, 1975—General Daniel "Chappie" James becomes first African-American four-star general.

May 28, 1980—Ninety-seven women graduate from the US Air Force Academy.

Timeline

April 14, 1986—Air Force launches Operation Eldorado Canyon against Libyan leader Muammar Qadhafi.

November 10, 1988—The Air Force reveals the existence of the F-117 stealth fighter.

June 10, 1989—Captain Jacqueline S. Parker becomes the first female pilot to graduate from US Air Force Test Pilot School.

December 20, 1989—Operation Just Cause begins to oust Manuel Noriega. It is the largest night-combat airdrop since the Normandy invasion in 1944.

August 2, 1990—Saddam Hussein's forces invade Kuwait.

August 7, 1990—Operation Desert Shield begins.

January 17, 1991—Operation Desert Storm begins with an all-out air assault.

February 28, 1991—Operation Desert Storm ends.

April 12, 1993—Operation Deny Flight, the air campaign against Bosnia-Herzegovina, begins.

August 6, 1993—Dr. Sheila E. Widnall becomes the first female armed services secretary.

February 10, 1994—Lieutenant Jeannie Flynn, the first female Air Force combat pilot, completes F-15 training.

February 3, 1995—Air Force Lieutenant Col. Eileen M. Collins becomes the first female space shuttle pilot.

September 3, 1996—The 11th Reconnaissance Squadron becomes first Air Force unit to operate Predator, an unmanned aerial vehicle.

March 24, 1999—Operation Allied Force begins in Kosovo and the B-2 makes its operational debut.

September 11, 2001—Terrorists strike the US by hijacking commercial aircraft and flying them into buildings.

October 7, 2001—The first military strike in the war on terrorism begins with Operation Enduring Freedom.

March 19, 2003—Operation Iraqi Freedom begins.

December 15, 2005—The F-22 plane is declared operationally ready.

December 30, 2006—Saddam Hussein is executed.

January 10, 2007—20,000 more US troops head to Iraq; surge begins.

July 22, 2008—Surge ends, leaving just under 147,000 American troops in Iraq.

August 31, 2010—President Obama declares an end to the seven-year American combat mission in Iraq.

December 18, 2011—Last US convoy leaves Iraq, ending US war in Iraq.

October 26, 2014—US and Britain end combat operations in Afghanistan.

February 13, 2015—Islamic State militants launch an attack on US airbase in Iraq.

CHAPTER NOTES

CHAPTER 1 Out of the Flames

1. 9/11 Commission, *9/11 Commission Report.* (New York: Barnes & Noble, 2006), p. 38.
2. Mark Tillman, as told to Dennis Wagner, “On 9/11, Air Force One Pilot’s Only Concern Was President Bush’s Safety.” *Arizona Republic,* September 11, 2011, <http://www.azcentral.com/news/articles/20110911 september-11-air-force-one-pilot.html> (February 6, 2015).
3. Ibid.
4. Ibid.
5. Ari Fleischer, *Taking Heat: The President, The Press and My Years in the White House* (New York: William Morrow, 2005), p. 141.
6. Ibid., p. 148.
7. Ibid., p. 150.

CHAPTER 2 The Wings of War

1. Robert Wohl, *A Passion for Wings: Aviation and the Western Imagination 1908–1918* (New Haven: Yale University Press, 1994), p. 11.
2. James L. Stokesbury, *A Short History of Air Power* (New York: William Morrow and Company, Inc., 1996), p. 13.
3. Herbert Molloy Mason, Jr., *The United States Air Force: A Turbulent History* (New York: Mason/Charter, 1976), p. 7.
4. Stokesbury, p. 14.
5. Ibid., p. 21.
6. James J. Hudson, *Hostile Skies: A Combat History of the American Air Service in World War I* (New York: Syracuse University Press, 1968), p. 3.
7. Ibid., pp. 4–5.
8. Mason, p. 67.
9. Ibid., p. 68.
10. Hudson, p. 139
11. Ibid., p. 186.
12. Ibid., p. 295.
13. Ibid., p. 299.
14. Mason, p. 74.

15. Ibid., p. 75.
16. Ibid., p. 76.
17. Ibid., p. 79.
18. Ibid., pp. 80, 82.
19. Ibid., p. 132.
20. Ibid., p. 141.
21. Edward Jablonski, *America in the Air War* (Alexandria, Va.: Time-Life Books, 1982), pp. 28, 30.
22. Kathleen T. Rhem, "Pentagon Hosts Salute to Hispanic World War II Veterans," *United States Department of Defense*, September 15, 2004, <http://www.defense.gov/news/newsarticle.aspx?id=25295> (February 9, 2015).
23. Mason, p. 207.

CHAPTER 3 Birth of an Independent Air Force

1. Walter J. Boyne, *Beyond the Wild Blue: A History of the US Air Force 1947–1997* (New York: St. Martin's Press, 1997), p. 33.
2. Herbert Molloy Mason, Jr., *The United States Air Force: A Turbulent History* (New York: Mason/Charter, 1976), p. 208.
3. Ivan Rendall, *Jet Combat From World War II to the Gulf War* (New York: The Free Press. 1997), p. 59.
4. James L. Stokesbury, *A Short History of Air Power* (New York: William Morrow and Company, Inc., 1996), p. 262.
5. Korean War Campaigns, "UN Offensive: September 16–November 2, 1950," *Air Force Historical Research Agency*, n.d., <http://www.afhra.af.mil/shared/media/document/AFD-090611-099.pdf> (February 9, 2015).
6. Korean War Campaigns, "Korea, Summer 1953: May l–July 27, 1953," *Air Force Historical Research Agency*, n.d., <http://www.afhra.af.mil/shared/media/document/AFD-090611-099.pdf> (February 9, 2015).
7. Cora Gibson Banta, "Memorializing a 'Forgotten War: The Korean War Veterans Memorial in Context," TCU Library, May 2014, p. 8, <https://repository.tcu.edu/handle/116099117/4524> (February 9, 2015).
8. Stokesbury, p. 278.
9. Ibid., pp. 281–282.
10. Ibid., p. 284.

11. Benjamin S. Lambeth, "NATO'S Air War For Kosovo: A Strategic and Operational Assessment," *Rand Corporation, Project Air Force* (Arlington, Va.: Rand), p. 87.
12. Ibid.
13. John A. Tirpak, "Two Decades of Stealth," *Air Force Magazine Online,* vol. 84, June 2001, <http://www.airforcemag.com/magazinearchive/pages/2001/june%202001/0601stealth.aspx> (February 9, 2015).

CHAPTER 4 Terror Hits Home

1. George W. Bush, "Address to a Joint Session of Congress and the American People," *The White House,* September 20, 2001, <http://georgewbush-whitehouse.archives.gov/news/releases/2001/09/20010920-8.html> (February 9, 2015).
2. Jim Garamone, "America Launches Strikes Against Al Qaeda, Taliban," *United States Department of Defense,* October 7, 2001, <http://www.defense.gov/news/newsarticle.aspx?id=44680> (February 9, 2015).
3. Cody H. Ramirez, "10 Year Anniversary of Strikes against Afghanistan," Whiteman Air Force Base, October 21, 2011, <http://www.whiteman.af.mil/news/story_print.asp?id=123276820> (February 9, 2015).
4. Linda D. Kozaryn, "Franks: Al Qaeda's Safe Harbor Is Gone," *United States Department of Defense,* February 7, 2002, <http://osd.dtic.mil/news/Feb2002/n02072002_200202072.html> (February 9, 2015).
5. Independent Election Commission of Afghanistan, *Afghanistan Presidential Election Results—2004,* n.d., <http://www.iec.org.af/public_html/Election%20Results%20Website/english/english.htm> (February 9, 2015).
6. George W. Bush, "President Says Saddam Hussein Must Leave Iraq Within 48 Hours," *The White House,* March 17, 2003, <http://georgewbush-whitehouse.archives.gov/news/releases/2003/03/20030317-7.html> (February 9, 2015).

CHAPTER 5 Today's Air Force

1. Jack Spencer, "The Facts About Military Readiness," Backgrounder #1394 on Missile Defense, The Heritage Foundation, September 15, 2000, <http://heritage.org/research/reports/2000/09/bg1394-the-facts-about-military-readiness> (February 11, 2015).

2. F. Whitten Peters and General Michael Ryan, "Air Expeditionary Forces," DOD Press Briefing," August 4, 1998, <http://fas.org/man/dod-101/usaf/unit/docs/eaftrans.pdf> (February 9, 2015).
3. C. Todd Lopez, "Standard AEF deployment length stretches to 120 days," Air Force Print News, June 4, 2004, <http://www.af.mil/News/ArticleDisplay/tabid/223/Article/136773/standard-aef-deployment-length-stretches-to-120-days.aspx> (February 10, 2015).
4. "Department of Defense Authorization for Appropriations for Fiscal Year 2004," S. Hrg. 108-241, Pt. 6, March 11, 19, 27, 2003, <http://psm.du.edu/media/documents/national_regulations/united_states/senate_and_house_committees/senate_armed_services/us_senate_armed_services_hearing_march_11_19_27_2003.pdf> (February 10, 2015).
5. VETS USERRA Fact Sheet 3, "Job Rights for Veterans and Reserve Component Members," US Department of Labor, n.d., <http://www.dol.gov/vets/programs/userra/userra_fs.htm> (February 10, 2015).
6. "About Air Force Reserve, " *Air Force Reserve,* n.d., <http://afreserve.com/about> (Februray 11, 2015).
7. Operation Noble Eagle, "Noble Eagle Overview," *Library of Congress,* March 22, 2003, <http://www.loc.gov/resource/POuaPOua5+GsWB9aN+980W2eg/ #?time=20030322144212> (February 10, 2015.
8. Deployment Health Clinical Center, "*Operation Joint Guardian – Kosovo Force (KFOR),*" n.d., <http://www.pdhealth.mil/deployments/allied_force/background.asp> (February 10-, 2015).

CHAPTER 6 Air Force Commands

1. "Air Combat Command," *Airman,* January 2005, <http://www.highbeam.com/doc/1G1-131432887.html> (February 10, 2015).
2. "Air Education and Training Command," *Airman,* January 2005, <http://www.highbeam.com/doc/1G1-131432888.html> (February 10, 2015).
3. "Air Force Reserve Command," *Airman,* January 2005, <http://www.highbeam.com/doc/1G1-131432890.html> (Februray 10, 2015).
4. "Air Force Special Operations Command," *Airman,* January 2005, <http://www.highbeam.com/doc/1G1-131432891.html> (February 10, 2015).
5. "Air Mobility Command," *Airman,* January 2005, <http://www.highbeam.com/doc/1G1-131432892.html> (February 10, 2015).

Chapter Notes

6. "Pacific Air Forces," *Airman*, January 2005, <http://www.highbeam.com/doc/1G1-131432893.html> (February 10, 2015).
7. "United States Air Forces in Europe," *Airman*, January 2005, <http://www.highbeam.com/doc/1G1-131432894.html> (February 10, 2015).
8. "Air National Guard," *Airman*, January 2005, <http://www.highbeam.com/doc/1G1-131432897.html> (February 10, 2015).

CHAPTER 7 Diversity in the Air Force

1. "United States Air Force Diversity Strategic Roadmap," Air Force Global Diversity Division, AF/A1DV, March 12, 2013, <http://www.af.mil/Portals/1/documents/diversity/diversity-strategic-roadmap.pdf> (February 12, 2015). Air Force Instruction 36-2706, "Military Equal Opportunity (MEO) Program," *Air Force e-Publishing*, July 29, 2004, <http://www.adr.af.mil/shared/media/document/AFD-070222-021.pdf> (February 10, 2015).
2. Valerie Moolman and the editors of Time-Life Books, *Women Aloft*, The Epic of Flight series, (Alexandria, Va.: Time-Life Books, 1981), p. 9.
3. Ibid., p. 135.
4. Ibid., p. 139.
5. Ibid.
6. Ibid., pp. 135, 141.
7. Ibid., p. 149.
8. Ibid., p. 153.
9. "Astronaut Bio: Eileen Collins," *National Aeronautics and Space Administration*, August 2005, <http://www.jsc.nasa.gov/Bios/htmlbios/collins.html> (February 10, 2015).
10. "Highlights in the History of Military Women," *Women in Military Service for America Memorial*, n.d., <http://womensmemorial.org/Education/timeline.html> (February 10, 2015).
11. Ibid.
12. Stephen Sherman, "The Tuskegee Airmen," June 29, 2011, <http://acepilots.com/usaaf_tusk.html> (February 10, 2015).
13. Walter J. Boyne, "Question Mark," *Air Force Magazine*, vol. 86, March 2003, p. 71, <http://www.dmairfield.com/The%20Question%20Mark.pdf> (February 10, 2015).

14. Carl Chance, "Hispanic American Aviators in World War II," July 17, 2011, <http://www.wingsoverkansas.com/history/a1416/> (February 10, 2015).

15. Department of Defense, "A Review of Data on Hispanic Americans," ROD SERIES PAMPHLET 98-4, n.d., <https://www.deomi.org/downloadableFiles/rodhsp98.pdf> (February 10, 2015).

16. "Duty Above All: Tech. Sgt. Sator 'Sandy' Sanchez," *National Museum of the United States Air Force*, August 28, 2009, <http://www.nationalmuseum.af.mil/factsheets/factsheet.asp?fsID=1666> (February 10, 2015).

17. Office of the Under Secretary of Defense (Personnel and Readiness), "Review of the Effectiveness of the Application and Enforcement of the Department's Policy on Homosexual Conduct in the Military," April 1998, <http://www.dod.mil/pubs/rpt040798.html> (February 10, 2015).

18. David F. Burrelli and Jody Feder, "Homosexuals and US Military Policy: Current Issues," CRS Report for Congress, July 22, 2009, <http://www.fas.org/sgp/crs/natsec/RL30113.pdf> (February 10, 2015).

19. "Air Force Personnel Demographics," *Air Force Personnel Center*, n.d., <http://www.afpc.af.mil/library/airforcepersonneldemographics.asp> (February 11, 2015).

CHAPTER 8 Air Force Life

1. Information taken from www.airforce.com and personal experiences.

CHAPTER 9 Donning the Air Force Blue

1. "Are You Ready for Basic Training?" US Air Force Fact Sheet, July 1, 2010, <http://www.basictraining.af.mil/library/factsheets/factsheet.asp?id=15718> (February 11, 2015).

2. Bruce D. Callander, "Warrior Week," *Air Force Magazine Online*, volume 82, December 1999, <http://www.airforcemag.com/MagazineArchive/Documents/1999/December%201999/1299warrior.pdf> (February 11, 2015).

3. "The Basis of True Strength Is Character," *United States Air Force Academy*, n.d., <http://www.academyadmissions.com/the-experience/character/honor-code/> (February 11, 2015).

Chapter Notes

4. "If You're Going to Compete, Give It Your All," *US Air Force Academy*, n.d., <http://www.academyadmissions.com/admissions/advice-to-applicants/all-applicants/academic-preparation/> (February 11, 2015).
5. Robert F. Collins, *Reserve Officer Training Corps: Campus Paths to Service Commissions* (New York: Rosen Publishing Group, 1986), p. ix.
6. Ibid., p. 56.
7. Ibid., pp. 76–77.
8. "OTS Home Page," *Officer Training School*, <http://ots.afoats.af.mil/> (January 1, 2006).

CHAPTER 10 Air Force Career Choices

1. "Vance Air Force Base Fact Sheet," August 2014, <http://www.vance.af.mil/shared/media/document/AFD-130213-025.pdf> (February 11, 2015).
2. "7th Space Warning Squadron," *US Air Force Fact Sheet*, n.d., <http://www.beale.af.mil/library/factsheets/factsheet.asp?id=3976> (February 11, 2015).
3. "9th Munitions Squadron," *US Air Force Fact Sheet*, February 25, 2014, <http://www.beale.af.mil/library/factsheets/factsheet.asp?id=3968> (February 11, 2015).

CHAPTER 11 Beyond the Wild Blue Horizon

1. Natalie Stanley, "SecAF, CSAF Discuss Future of the Air Force," *Secretary of the Air Force Public Affairs Command Information*, January 15, 2015, <http://www.af.mil/News/ArticleDisplay/tabid/223/Article/560283/secaf-csaf-discuss-the-future-of-the-air-force.aspx> (February 13, 2015).
2. John P. Jumper, "Toward New Air and Space Horizons," 2005 Air Force Association Air Warfare Symposium," February 18, 2005, <http://www.highbeam.com/doc/1G1-133904501.html> (February 11, 2015).
3. Melanie Streeter, "Space Integrates Air Forces to Win Wars," *Air Force Print News*, February 17, 2004, <http://www.af.mil/News/ArticleDisplay/tabid/223/Article/137597/space-integrates-air-forces-to-win-wars.aspx> (February 11, 2015).

4. Austin Carter, "New Squadron Trains for Space-Based Aggression," *Space Daily*, October 25, 2000, <http://www.spacedaily.com/news/milspace-00q.html> (February 11, 2015).
5. Richard J. Newman, "The Little Predator That Could," *Air Force Magazine Online*, vol. 85, March 2002, <http://www.airforcemag.com/MagazineArchive/Pages/2002/March%202002/0302predator.aspx> (February 1, 2015).
6. Torri Ingalsbe, "AF Chief of Staff: Call to the Future," Secretary of the Air Force Public Affairs Command Information, February 13, 2015, <http://www.af.mil/News/ArticleDisplay/tabid/223/Article/566082/af-chief-of-staff-call-to-the-future.aspx> (February 13, 2015).

GLOSSARY

ace—Military pilot who shoots down five or more enemy aircraft.

Air Expeditionary Force (AEF)—Air Force combat and support forces are organized into ten AEFs to respond to recurring missions around the world.

Air Force One—The president's aircraft based at Andrews AFB.

air refueling—Aircraft receiving fuel from another aircraft in mid-flight.

base exchange (BX)—Shopping facility on most bases that resembles a department store.

blockade—The blocking by military forces of access to a place in order to prevent the entry of goods.

close air support—Air action against hostile targets close to friendly ground or naval forces requiring detailed integration of fire and movement.

coalition—A temporary alliance of distinct parties, persons, or states for joint action.

collateral damage—Unintentional damage to things or people in the vicinity of an intended target.

Combat Air Patrols—Aerial fighting positions over a target or location.

deploy—To be sent overseas to support a military operation.

ethnic—Of a racial gropup or member of such a group.

joint operation—A mission or exercise involving more than one military service.

munitions—A weapon like a bomb or missile.

precision-guided munitions—Weapons guided to their targets by satellites or radar.

psychological operations—Using information against the enemy to destroy its morale or will to fight.

reconnaissance—Collecting information or intelligence on an enemy.

rules of engagement (ROE)—Legal regulations in warfare.

squadron—Basic military unit made up of multiple flights.

sortie—One flight by an aircraft.

stealth—An airplane's ability to evade detection by radar.

strategy—The planning and directing of the whole operation of a campaign or war.

ultimatum—A final warning or order.

FURTHER READING

Books

Grayson, Robert. *The US Air Force. Essential Library of the US Military.* Edina, Minn.: Abdo Publishing, 2014.

Green, Michael. *The United States Air Force.* North Mankato, Minn.: Capstone Publishing, 2013.

Lusted, Marcia Amidon. *Air Commandos: Elite Operations. Military Special Ops.* Minneapolis, Minn.: Lerner Books, 2013.

Miller, Adam. *US Air Force True Stories: Tales of Bravery.* North Mankato, Minn.: Capstone Publishing, 2015.

Stentiford, Barry. *Tuskegee Airmen.* Santa Barbara, Calif.: ABC-CLIO-Greenwood, 2012.

Whiting, Jim. *US Special Forces: Air Force Special Operations Command.* Mankato, Minn.: The Creative Company, 2015.

Yenne, Bill. *Hap Arnold: The General Who Invented the Air Force.* Washington, D.C.: Regnery History, 2013.

Web Sites

academyadmissions.com/

The Air Force Academy Admissions site provides valuable information about joining the Air Force for prospective applicants and their parents.

lackland.us/

This is the official site of Lackland's Basic Military Training.

af.mil

The US Air Force's official site is full of history and news.

Movies

Pearl Harbor. Directed by Michael Bay. Burbank, Calif.: Walt Disney Pictures, 2001.

Red Tails. Directed by Anthony Hemingway. Los Angeles, Calif.: 20th Century Fox, 2012.

The Airman's Medal is awarded for heroism.

INDEX

Index